# When God Says No

## Judith Briles

Fleming H. Revell
A Division of Baker Book House Co
Grand Rapids, Michigan 49516

Published by Fleming H. Revell
a division of Baker Book House Company
P.O. Box 6287, Grand Rapids, MI 49516-6287

Previously published in 1990 by Word Publishing

Printed in the United States of America

### Library of Congress Cataloging-in-Publication Data

Briles, Judith.
   When God says no / Judith Briles.
     p.    cm.
   Originally published: Dallas, Tex. : Word Pub., c1990.
   ISBN 0-8007-5618-5 (pbk.)
   1. Briles, Judith. 2. Suffering—Religious aspects—Christianity.
3. Theodicy. 4. Christian biography—United States. I. Title.
   [BR1725.B6835A3 1997]
   248.8′6—dc21
                                              96-47560

In memory of
*Frank* and *Billy*

# *Acknowledgments*

This book was in my heart for many years. Friends and family would ask me—did I really want to write about such painful times in my life, about some of my failures, exposing myself to old hurts and wounds? Many that had already healed?

The answer was yes . . . and no. As I settled in to write about my sons and other significant events of my past, I learned a lot about myself. I had healed, I had grown, and I could reach out and give to others, with no expectations in return.

*When God Says No* has been introspective for me. The friends, family, and buyers who have read it have been overwhelmed by its message. The letters and calls I have received have been too numerous to even try to count. Many have bought the book for friends who are in pain.

Thank you to my family—John, Sheryl, Shelley, Frankie, Terry, and Joyce. Without their love, encouragement, and support, my journey in bringing this book to you would have been extremely difficult. To Jean Hollands, Alan Leavens, and John Snyder, who were there unconditionally when it seemed the darkest; and to Linda Holland, who saw the power and need to rebirth this message.

All of us have been a team . . . a gift to and for each other.

# *Contents*

# Introduction

Standing in front of my bay window with my youngest daughter perched on my hip, I watched my six-year-old son wolf down his lunch—a peanut butter and jelly sandwich—as he sat on the curb waiting for the school bus. It was 8:10 A.M.

Frank's buddy, Robin, was matching him bite for bite. The two boys closed their lunch boxes, walked across the street, opened the door and Frank announced, "We have quit school. It's too long, too hard and not fair." Shy Robin nodded his head in agreement.

Sheryl thought it was great that her big brother had come back from the bus stop. At three, she idolized him. Anything that Frank did was OK with her. It wasn't always so with me. Having your six-year-old state that he was dropping out of school was not the ideal way to start any day.

Making new sandwiches for both, I told them in my best kick-'em-in-the-pants voice, "Life is often too long, too hard and unfair. Take these sandwiches and march out and wait for your bus. Now!"

Thirteen years later, Frank's six-year-old voice permeated my entire being. Frank was dead. An accident. That Labor Day weekend of 1983 touched thousands of lives. Ten of Frank's friends, including his younger sister Sheryl, were with him when he fell twenty feet from the old Dumbarton Bridge into the chilly waters of the San Francisco Bay. This was the first tragedy that any of them had ever experienced. It was a tragedy that would reach out and engulf others —parents, teens and the media.

This was not the first time death had touched me so closely. Twelve years earlier, Frank's younger brother, Billy, had died. Although the feelings, the responses, the impact of each was so different on family, friends and the community, there was a common thread that wove the two events together.

I felt just like six-year-old Frank—life was too long, too hard and certainly not fair. There was no way that I wanted anything to do with anyone, especially riding on that bus known as life. Little did I know that Frank was about to take me on the bus ride of a lifetime—that he would introduce me to the three most valuable gifts I would ever receive.

### The Gifts

With *Frank's first gift,* I received a newness of life, of purpose. This gift was one of a renewal of spirituality. God had taken a back seat in my life for too long . . . always there, but rarely acknowledged on my part.

The door to my belief in Jesus Christ had been set ajar when I was a little girl of seven. None of the members of my immediate family knew I went to church, that I had even had myself baptized. In looking back, the church protected me from an unhappy home, but I grew up and eventually, away.

Gradually, over the years I had allowed the door

to close, especially after a painfully bitter divorce. Only a crack existed. That is, it did until September of 1983. Then the door blew open, ripped from the hinges and was gone. It no longer existed.

*The second gift* was equally as important. It got me in touch with who I am and what my values are. The second gift also taught me how important my voice is, how important it is to stand up and be counted and how important it is to reach out, no matter how lonely, how hurt and how angry one is.

*The third gift* wasn't as buried as the first or second. Frank left me his "little kid spirit." I didn't want to do anything unless I could have fun. Oh, hard work wasn't eliminated—that will always be there. But now, I can always find the irony, the humor of any situation, no matter how negative or how big the *no* is or was.

Each of these gifts was wrapped, but all were packaged together with a huge bow, on which was inscribed *When God Says No*—the title of this book.

### The Bus Ride of Life

Contained within these pages is a highly personal journey beginning with my very first question: *Why?* Why did Frank have to die? In the first chapter, this question is explored at the beginning level. Through asking this question, I discovered that there was a time to ask this very important question—but equally important, a time to move away from why.

My bus ride continues in the second chapter with a journey through the *noes,* the *yeses,* and the *not yet's* of God. In a very real sense, God does answer our questions—though not all of our questions—with replies that can sometimes seem obtuse. Or negative.

But behind these answers there is hope—and often a *yes*!

Riding along into chapter three, I will take a closer look at what nourishing a *no* can do to a person—and how to extract yourself from the muck and mire of a *no*. How to get "unstuck," to move forward into the future. There is hope!

Patience is the key that unlocks the journey's door in the next chapter. More often than we like, our *yeses* come out of waiting. And waiting. And waiting. But through waiting patiently there are rewards that can be discovered. We'll discover some of those together.

Next I delve deeper into this waiting process to discover how to move out of the turmoil of waiting into a place of assurance. Chapter five is an exploration of this moving forward process on the bus ride of life. Building a foundation of assurance is the preparation for what follows: How to find faith.

Chapter six moves into a deeper spiritual journey. It takes us to the land of faith—a place where one can tangibly perceive that "If God is on our side, who can ever be against us?" (Romans 8:31). Faith is an important part of the journey of discovering the *yeses* behind God's *noes* because without faith, you'll never believe there are any *yeses*.

It is here, in these last three chapters, that the three gifts Frank's death brought to me become crystal clear. It is here in chapter seven that Frank's first gift—the gift of renewed spirituality—begins to take shape.

Frank's second gift, the gift of learning to stand up and be counted, emerges in chapter seven. Here I discuss finding a spiritual vision. With the enormous pain that was felt, incredible doors have opened—doors that I might never have seen and doors that would have been blockaded if I hadn't let a *spiritual vision* carry me, if I hadn't put myself in God's arms.

The book concludes with a chapter on miracles—*they can and do happen!* This is where Frank's third gift to me, his "little kid spirit," comes alive. Just as a butterfly emerges from a caterpillar's cocoon, miracles emerge from the ugly scars in our lives. These last three chapters tie up the package of this book—my gift to you.

Most of us are so hurt and angry when we fall into life's pitfalls, that we miss the yeses in our lives. What I have learned and certainly experienced over the past seven years is that God does leave a *yes,* and one is often found behind each *no,* which is the basis of this book. I hope that in these pages, you will find the comfort, the hope—the miracle—that you need. As you journey with me on the bus ride through the lessons I've learned, may you discover your *yes,* the *yes* that is lurking . . . waiting to be invited in.

# 1

# Moving Away
# from *Why*

**W**hy? And why Frank? This only happens to people on the news. Other people. Yet this time the airwaves were brimming with reports about *my* family, *my* son, *my* life—a cruel reminder that it was happening to me. Little did I know that such an ordinary Friday night would open up a Pandora's box of "Whys?"

As I finished the dinner dishes, the usual Friday night noises were in the background. Sheryl, at sixteen, still had the phone attached to her ear in the family room. She was planning for the evening activities as well as the remainder of the long Labor Day weekend ahead with the shared friends she had with her older brother. Frank was nineteen and still very much a kid—his latest toy was the new kitten, Cashmere. He had brought her home for Sheryl when hers had been hit by a car a few weeks earlier. All three of the kids laughed at Cashmere's antics as Frank got her to jump higher and higher, reaching for a bright red ribbon.

Shelley was taking a breather from her school books and just enjoying the craziness that always seemed to surround our household. She had been working part time while carrying a full academic load at college. She was saving money, planning for when she would finally have a place of her own, always brainstorming with friends on who would move out first, and declaring total independence from the home front. All these items were foremost in her game plan. At twenty-one, Shelley had always been the most responsible of the kids. There were times when I wished she could be as silly as Frank allowed himself to be and occasionally as irresponsible as Sheryl had proven in the past.

Dishes completed and the phone silent, the kids continued with their plans for the evening. Since it was Daylight Saving Time, they would meet at the drive-in movies for the latest thriller around nine. Frank remarked that he would be in shortly after midnight since he had to open the gas station where he worked at eight the following morning. He would bring Sheryl home with him. Shelley decided to stay in that night and would meet her friends the next morning.

My husband John arrived home shortly after Frank and Sheryl left with some of their friends who had already dropped by. John was up to his eyeballs getting ready for the new year at Menlo College where he taught and served as Chairman of the Science and Engineering Department. With the influx of new students, we rarely saw him before nightfall as each new fall term began. Tomorrow was his birthday and we had plans to celebrate it with a few friends that evening.

Relishing the quiet of the evening and making a conscious choice not to do any studying that weekend for the doctorate I was working on, John and I decided to escape to the Friday night movie on TV and our favorite bowl of popcorn.

Turning the TV off after the movie was over and leaving the porch and hallway lights on, we said good night to Shelley and retreated to our end of the house.

At one in the morning I awoke suddenly. Something was amiss. I rolled out of bed and wandered down the hallway checking on each of the kids. I wondered how many times I had followed in these steps, the steps of the "mommy walk"—the steps that every mother traces when her inner self says, "Go."

The check-off began. Shelley was asleep in her room, her door still closed. Sheryl's bedroom door was wide open—I mentally made a note to bean her for being out this late, whatever beaning would mean to me when I saw her in the morning. Frank's door was closed. Assuming he was in, I was relieved. Remembering his remark that he had to open the gas station at eight in the morning, I knew that getting up early was not on his list of favorite things to do.

Letting one of our dogs and two of the cats out, and the other dog in, I returned to bed. As I dozed off, my mind told me that it must have been the sound of the animals wanting in and out that had awakened me a few minutes earlier. Otherwise, Frank would have wakened me if there were any problems with Sheryl. Something in me didn't agree. I still felt unsettled. It was 1:10 A.M.

The clock that hung in our living room struck three times. Sitting straight up, I felt Sheryl's presence at the foot of my side of the bed. Leaping out, I moved toward her, grabbed her wrists and without realizing what I was saying, the words tumbled out of my mouth, "What do you mean Frank is in the morgue?"

She was crying and said, "No, Mom, just come," as she took my hand and led me down the hallway that was now brightly lit. John trailed behind me and as our threesome passed Shelley's room, her door opened and she joined us.

Not knowing where Sheryl was leading our nocturnal train, we entered the family room. I first saw the police car through the house windows, and then my eyes met those of the lone policeman standing in the middle of the room.

"Mrs. Briles? I'm sorry, there has been an accident." My mind tumbled with the news of Frank's fall. My world froze. I was suspended in death's grip as life continued around me. My mind refocused to catch his parting remark: "The Coast Guard will keep searching. I'll call you as soon as there's news."

There was no more sleep as the remainder of the night unfolded. Each of us sat silently with our own tormented thoughts. The radio was turned to the local news station, as we hoped, yet feared to hear some scrap of information.

Automatically, I made pots of coffee and tea and set them on the coffee table. I found a legal pad and pen that could be kept at arm's length ready to jot down any thoughts or news. Shelley and Sheryl were wrapped in blankets at opposite ends of the couch, both losing patience as each hour passed and no mention was made of their brother's fall. Each half hour John checked in with the State Police—"Had the Coast Guard found anything yet?" Each believed that just maybe, just maybe, Frank would be found . . . alive.

Except me. I knew that Frank was dead. When I felt Sheryl at the foot of our bed I had known it. Unknown to me, my "mommy walk" was a forewarning. The very same moments I was checking which doors were open and which were closed, Frank had slipped quietly to his death.

Sheryl filled in the bits and pieces of what had happened. Everyone had gone to the movies as planned.

Bored with the double bill feature, they left at midnight and convened at the local A.M.-P.M. store. The group decided that they would drive out to the old Dumbarton Bridge and climb on it—something that several of them had done in the past for "kicks." With a twelve-pack of beer purchased and adrenaline flowing, ten kids excitedly set out on their daring adventure.

Not all of them climbed. Sheryl stayed down. It was too scary for her. She called out for the boys to come down—"Let's go!" She wanted to go home. Gradually each descended. Frank was one of the last down. He had climbed before, but his friend Eric was doing it for the first time and was descending above Frank.

As Frank got closer to the bottom, he stopped and waited for Eric to catch up. He took a step. It was his last. The kids heard a thud, then a splash. They rushed over to the side of the roadway and peered into the bay. A cassette tape from Frank's tape player bobbed on top of the water—the only remaining evidence of his fall.

There was confusion. "What's that?" Night's shadows hid faces. "Who's missing?" Should someone jump in to find out? "It's Frank! He's fallen."

Sheryl jumped in one of the cars, fish-tailed, squashing the twelve-pack which lay unopened on the ground and flew like a bullet to the toll bridge. Surely there would be someone there who could help, who would know what to do. Who would fix everything.

It seemed to take forever. At 1:12 A.M. she reached the toll booth. At first the operator didn't believe her—he thought it was just kids and their pranks. Because of her persistence, he got in touch with the State Police who in turn called in the Coast Guard, requesting both boats and helicopters.

Frank's friends were zombies, almost catatonic. None could believe the nightmare in which they found themselves immersed. Sheryl couldn't conceive that her brother was dead and was convinced he would be found hanging on to a piling or clinging to a log.

After an hour and a half the police escorted the kids home. Sheryl lingered—hoping. She was the last to leave the site, she and the lone policeman.

Back in our living room we waited, dreading a phone call yet wishing it would come. The police called a few minutes after 6 A.M. The Coast Guard had called off their search for the time being. We didn't know what that meant. Later we learned that it meant they had given up. Sheryl tearfully questioned, "I guess there is no hope then." I wish I could have said yes, that there was always hope. But I couldn't and didn't. There wasn't.

In contrast to my clear understanding that Frank was gone, were the muddled thoughts which fogged my mind. Why did this happen? And to one so young? With so much to look forward to? So many dreams to realize? To Frank who had finally gotten his act together?

On top of that, as though a chapter had never been completed, all the old aches of Billy's death resurfaced. Billy was my other son—Frank's longed-for baby brother who died in 1971 after living only a few days.

The impact of each death was so different. Billy's death affected only the immediate family. There had been no service—I couldn't even bear to read the cards that were sent from friends.

This time it was in the news. It was public. This time there were ten close friends there at the time Frank died. This time I couldn't withdraw into a room for three months, painting and listening to records.

This time a service had to be held. This time I couldn't escape the nagging questions. And this time I had to have answers.

One thing became unmistakably clear. My life had taken a dramatic turn—whether I liked it or not. And with this turn I would never be the same. As days turned into weeks, weeks into months, I found that I could either let myself die with my loss of Frank or discover a new reason to live.

Although no answers came quickly, I searched for hope—not the vain optimism which had kept Sheryl hoping that somehow Frank would be found alive—but another one. *Real* hope. The kind of hope I realized could only be found through a spiritual journey. I somehow expected that the bus which arrived at my doorstep when Frank died would take me on. Reluctantly, almost without choice, I boarded that bus.

## Why, Why, Why?

Our first temptation when confronted with tragedy, any tragedy, is to ask why. John's father, who was undergoing radiation treatments for cancer of the throat, was stunned. Ed felt it wasn't fair that so young a life was gone. Why not he? He was 86. He had lived a full life. Why not the ones who were already ill? Why a healthy child? Why Frank?

The phone rang constantly. Each call brought the same questions—how and why?

How could I answer those questions? They were my own. I thought of Frank and how his life was taking shape. Frank was growing up, at last. He was making plans for the future. He had saved $2,000 to buy the motorcycle of his dreams—papers were to be drawn up

Tuesday morning—less than 72 hours after his death. It was the first banking day after Labor Day. I had convinced him to use his savings as collateral for a loan, establishing him as a credit-abiding member of society! He was even forewarning his younger friends that it was stupid to drop out of high school—they needed to continue with their education.

Frank had taken a lot of years to arrive at this new-found maturity, taking side roads along the way. We had removed him from the house twice in his brief life. The first came when he got involved with a group of kids whose influence was negative with a capital N. A new school, boarding away for six months, finally broke the spell. Years later, when we experienced similar problems with his younger sister, he suggested that we do the same with her. He had said he hated me then, but he thanked me as he looked back. Whew—it was heady stuff for a parent finally to hear her actions validated.

The second time was when he was eighteen. We had a rule that if graduation had occurred, then each kid could stay in the house rent free if he or she was going to college full time. Otherwise, rent had to be paid and a full-time job obtained. Or move out. Frank didn't believe me. Well, not at first. He thought we were kidding. We weren't. We changed the locks, put his clothes in his truck and let him know that he was not welcome. This happened only after we gave repeated warnings that D-Day was approaching. He threatened to sleep on the front lawn—what would the neighbors think? I told him I didn't care what they thought. I made his favorite dinner—the last supper. And I had told him that this was it—he was on his own after his last meal. He laughed. Then he got mad—we actually weren't bluffing.

Frank slept in his truck for three nights, then moved in with a friend. The friend's mother called, I explained the circumstances, what our rule was, and suggested that she charge rent. Frank wasn't welcome at our house. Within ten days he called me wanting to make an appointment. He had a job, could he come home and rejoin our family? Yes, with conditions—out came the contract—duties, rights, privileges and paying his share. Amazingly, Frank grew up. He was on his way to becoming a responsible, productive adult.

So why now? Why did this happen when Frank had begun to make positive choices in his life? Why didn't God prevent the accident from happening? It wasn't as if Frank was a bad kid. We weren't perfect, but we were good people—people who had lived by the Golden Rule. Other people got their miracles . . . why didn't we?

Even as I asked these questions I began to understand that *Why* was only one side of a two-sided question. On the other side of the coin was the stark question, *Why not me?* It's not as though I deserved a corner on good luck. Look around. Tragedy strikes without warning and without any relationship to a person's moral character. Chaste women are the innocent victims of rape. Godly couples are the unsuspecting parents of a retarded or handicapped child. Loving parents lose their children every year through drownings or car accidents. Unsuspecting children and adults contract AIDS. In reality, life's simply not fair.

The question then becomes, why isn't life fair? If God could prevent these things from happening, is He cruel and sadistic? Does He find some kind of perverse pleasure in our suffering? Is He a master game player? And if He can't prevent these things from happening, can we then claim He is all powerful? Just what makes Him tick?

Some would try to ennoble our suffering by saying that God is trying to "teach us a lesson"—or that we are somehow "special" because He has "chosen" us to suffer a certain fate. I have heard these phrases more times than I care to count. Being taught a lesson or being special or chosen to be the recipient of bum luck, tragedy, is alien to me. All were unsatisfactory answers.

As Frank's mother, I certainly understood that I sometimes had to choose an unpopular means of discipline. After all, I did kick him out of the house. But it was a lesson in "tough love" that was for his benefit. After all, most parents must choose to be a parent rather than a "buddy." The punishment was appropriate for the crime—his blasé attitude that led to the ignoring of our house rules.

In this instance, there was no crime to relate to Frank's death. It was arbitrary. Somehow I couldn't believe in an arbitrary God who would kill my child— or allow my child to be killed—to teach him or me or my family a lesson. What would the lesson have been? You shouldn't have stayed out so late? You should have been more careful not to lose your footing? I should have been a better mother and then Frank would have known better than to go climbing out on a dangerous bridge?

On the other hand, if being "chosen" by God to suffer the death of my child was an answer to my *whys* then to my way of thinking, there are plenty of other candidates out there. Let Him choose someone else. Not me. Not us. I'd rather have Frank with me than to be writing this book about my struggles to find purpose in my pain.

No, the God of love whom I had been taught about as a child sneaking off to church, the God of compassion when I had been baptized to serve, the God of my memories was a God who stilled the seas, who healed the sick, who forgave the sinful and who walked on this earth to identify with our pain—not create it.

There's a passage in the Old Testament, Deuteronomy 29:29 which says, "There are secrets which the Lord your God has not revealed to us, but these words which he has revealed are for us and our children to obey forever." There are things we may never understand in this life—secret things—that God never gives us an answer to. But there are things that He reveals to us. And those are the areas where we can search for answers. It is in that search that God promises He can be found. "For I know the plans I have for you, says the Lord. They are plans for good and not for evil, to give you a future and a hope. In those days when you pray, I will listen. You will find me when you seek me, if you look for me in earnest. Yes, says the Lord, I will be found by you" (Jeremiah 29:11–14).

Here God tells us that He doesn't want us to experience evil things. His plans, His hopes, His dreams for us are for peace. When we search for Him, He promises to give us that peace.

Soon I began to understand that focusing on the why would prevent me from ever moving on to my place of peace. In a very real sense, there were no answers for my whys. Asking why can only cloud the past, the present and the future for anyone. *Why*, joined by its paralyzing mate, *If only*, haunts all of us who have experienced misfortune, hurt, loneliness, fear or sickness. When you flip the coin and the question becomes, *Why not me?*, then you are ready to move forward to experience and explore the future rather than being plagued, haunted and embittered by the past.

My future has been unalterably changed by Frank's death. My thoughts, my passions, my lifestyle will never be what they were before his tragic fate. But now I know that I no longer feel the need to ask why—not because it's wrong to ask, but because I've grown beyond that question. And growing beyond means I'm not stuck in the past. For me, *why* was the open door to a deeper and richer understanding of life. *Why* was the question that helped me to begin to understand God's noes, but more importantly, His yeses. Letting go of *why* opened up fantastic doors—doors that I never knew existed. These doors have allowed me to look back at my past experiences—the good times and the bad—and be able to say, "I have a good life."

# 2

# No, Yes
# and Not Yet

Something's wrong. Help! Don't let something be wrong with my baby. I can't stand the pain any longer. *Breathe. Breathe.* He'll be OK. It'll be fine. *Breathe.* My babies always come early. What's wrong? What's taking so long? Labor was so quick with each of my babies. Sheryl, my third, had a mind of her own. We barely made it to the hospital. My husband dropped me off and I was whisked to the labor room. With no help, Sheryl arrived—just she and I. And God.

I want this baby out. *One more push.* He's here. It's a boy! A boy! Ten fingers. Ten toes. He's even got hair! A first! It was so exciting! Six pounds, seven ounces. He's crying. He sounds great. The nurses check reflexes and breathing. Perfect score: ten. He's perfect— my fourth perfect baby! But something's still wrong . . . with me. The afterbirth isn't coming. I can't push it out. I'm so tired. But at least my baby's OK. He's OK . . . isn't he?

Billy wasn't OK. Two days later he died. He was premature—five weeks early. His was such a short life. His lungs just weren't ready—Hyaline-Membrane disease. Because his weight was so normal and his test scores came out so good, the doctors and nurses didn't recognize the danger he was in. Billy gasped for his last breath, as his lungs collapsed and he died. It was all so unnecessary. So preventable. So unfair. Yet for whatever reason, God allowed it. He could have said *yes,* but for some mysterious reason, He said *no.*

It didn't help when the hospital staff wouldn't let me see or hold my baby. It didn't help when they never told me what to do or what to expect. My body, my mind, my heart, my soul—all were prepared to nurse and nurture and love this little boy. How do you deal with a body that is prepared for a baby when there is no baby? No one told me. All the doctor said was no sex for six weeks. I went home empty-handed, empty-hearted. So alone.

Shelley, Frank and Sheryl all came running to see their baby brother. They didn't know he had died. No one had told them—another task for my empty heart to deal with. There was no baby brother to show them.

I was furious with the doctor and angry with the hospital. I never wanted to set foot in that hospital or see that doctor again. But I didn't feel anger toward God. Somehow, that didn't hit me as an option. It's just that this nagging question, "Why?" kept coming up. Why did *my* baby have to die? Why weren't *my* prayers answered? Why did God say *no?* My perfect, innocent baby boy.

Deep in my heart, I buried my questions. That is, until Frank's death. But when Frank died, I needed to know that there was some reason for all the pain, all the tragedy I had suffered. Certainly others had suffered more, but somehow I didn't believe I deserved all this. Somehow I didn't believe a good and loving God could overlook the tragedies in our lives and be unaffected. Uncaring. Or worse yet—impotent.

The anguish I felt was no different than the pain shared by any parent—including biblical parents. In the Old Testament the poignant and familiar story of

David appears. After taking Bathsheba and having her husband killed, David pleads with God to save his baby. The baby didn't sin. David fasts and prays. He repents and humbles himself before God. Yet this innocent life, this precious baby . . . dies. God said *no*. Quietly, decisively, inexplicably, *no*.

### Noes Lead to Yes

It was this way until I discovered a mysterious truth—that behind every *no* lurks a *yes*. And that *yes* is woven into the fabric of a plan that reaches far beyond our own lives.

That truth unfolded one Sunday morning as I sat in a sanctuary full of much-pained people in the summer of 1985. The church I belonged to had been driven apart by a series of events involving the senior pastor—a man who had been so instrumental in reinvolving me in the church. He was a man I barely recognized that day, after having known him for two years. He was on a path of "self-destruct." A man I once loved for his caring and giving had vanished into his shell, an alien.

Our fellowship had been ripped apart. Member pitted against member. Personal and financial information was bandied about by the congregation. As stewardship chair I was sickened to learn that records I felt such a responsibility for were leaked to others. I was pained by the depths of anger, fear, hostility—even hatred—that permeated the air.

Where was God? He couldn't possibly be here, there, not with us. Yet He was. The day before, a special meeting of the congregation had been called. We had just finished an intensive multi-week counseling/ evaluation by a group that specializes in conflicts within the church. This was an understatement, to say the least, with what had been going on at our church.

The results were to be presented to all. The night before, our Session had met with both pastors and members from the Presbytery. Both pastors had decided to tender their resignations. As the meeting started, the majority of the congregation didn't know that both were to leave.

The past several months had been grueling—I couldn't imagine what had been in my mind when I accepted the nomination to the Session of our church. There I found myself, an elected elder, hated by a group within the church, party to information that was privileged and could not be exposed. My mind played gymnastics—"if only they knew the truth."

For months I had dialogued with God—why was I here? Why was I in the midst of such turmoil? Why, when my wounds from Frank's death were so open, so raw? The answer was always the same, "You are needed . . . you must be there."

During this period I can remember driving home from the airport hating the position I was in—seeing "friends" destroy their friendships as they were pitted against each other. But the internal dialogue continued, "You must be there," I wanted to resign as several of the other elders had done. I wanted out. I was being pulled apart by people I cared for. I felt as I had when Frank died—so vulnerable, so alone, so hurt.

My inner voice continued, "I need you there. Stay." Tears streamed down my face as I drove from the airport. But I made the commitment to hang in there—hatred, pain and all.

On that Sunday an amazing thing happened. An Associate Pastor had been sent to fill the void—to lead our services and communion. An incredible event happened. The title of his sermon was the title of this book—"When God Says No." Words were put to my anguish. That sermon changed my life and those of hundreds of others. For the first time an incredible feeling of peace descended from the rafters, enveloping all who sat there that morning. God, through Dr. John Snyder, now pastor at Trinity Presbyterian Church in Fresno, California, had done the impossible. John Snyder stayed with our congregation for over a year. He brought the depth of his knowledge, caring, spirituality and healing skills to our small town in Northern California. It was a miracle for me . . . for so many. Through his sermons I began to discover the *yeses* behind God's *noes.*

As every parent knows, child raising can be an incredible challenge. One illustration John Snyder used was so simple, and so logical—that of a mother telling her child *no.* No caring mother would knowingly want her child in an unsafe or potentially dangerous situation. Rather, she says *no.* No pleading, begging or tantrums can change her mind. Behind the *no* is a *yes*— *yes* as in, "I don't want you to hurt yourself. I care for you. I love you."

In turn, when God gave the Israelites the law, He conveyed it with a *yes* behind His stern *no.* "And now, Israel, what does the Lord your God require of you except to listen carefully to all he says to you, and to obey *for your own good* the commandments I am giving you today, and to love him and to worship him with all your hearts and souls?" (Deuteronomy 10:12, 13, emphasis mine). There was a list of rules. They were not rules for rule's sake, not to be harsh. Rather, they were rules that would be filled with benefits for the God's children.

Through John Snyder's explanations of these truths I was able to move forward through the bitter struggles of our church to a deeper understanding of life's *noes*. All my questions weren't answered, all my *whys* weren't put to rest, but I was able to begin putting the puzzle back together in spite of the missing pieces. When John accepted a position with another church, his work was done. He had been able to heal several immense wounds. Today he is missed by many in our church. In fact, many of us travel to his new church every once in a while to get a "John Snyder fix."

He brought phenomenal wisdom with his sermons, his insights. The Reverend Dr. John Snyder has been one of God's miracles for me . . . as well as for so many others.

### Historical Noes

The newspapers are laden with stories, present and past, of the *noes* that make up history. As I write this, the media is revisiting the history of the French Revolution. That event which happened two centuries ago still divides the hearts of people. Two hundred years ago the people rose up and rebelled against the French aristocracy. It's more than an historical fact—it's a celebrated event! In 1989 the people of France celebrated the Revolution that brought freedom to their land. Emotions ran high. Today, some have wanted to bring back the aristocracy—the "good old days." Others have objected to celebrating such a bloody "head-rolling" event. Still others have felt that it is necessary to recognize the importance of this nation-changing event, simply because it's part of their history.

Any viewpoint produces reactions. You can be assured that many of those reactions just mentioned have been passed down from one generation to the next. For good or for evil, the French Revolution changed lives and brought liberty to a nation of people. Forever, the revolution will be woven into the fabric of French society and will continue affecting future generations. Consequently, the French Revolution is still alive in the hearts and minds of many of the French people today.

There are two important points to remember in this. First, what was evil to the aristocracy was liberating to an entire people. Behind the bloody *no* of two hundred years ago lay a future of independence. Second, what happens in history is an intricate part of our lives today. History affects the present. Just look at the French Revolution. Just look at Eastern Europe. We are interconnected. We are part of a larger picture—a larger plan. We are part of a continuum. Therefore, the events in our lives have greater significance than our immediate sojourn here on earth. There is a vantage point and perspective that we don't have. We may not see anything positive being created from bad news, pain and suffering. Hindsight, however, allows us to see that there are times when what happens to us happens for a greater good.

Don't get me wrong. I'm not suggesting we're "pawns" in the "game" of life. Neither am I suggesting that some greater good justifies evil or that God was behind the French Revolution. What I am proposing is that there may be instances when what is perceived as an immediate evil can work for a greater good. I'm also saying that what happens in our lives is significant—beyond the scope of our own lives. Behind every *no* lies a *yes*. What it means is this: In the overall fabric and plan of God, He hasn't lost control.

## Life's Tapestry

If each of us lives to be 75 we will share 25,550 days earthbound. I can't pretend to understand all the purposes of God, but I do know we are all inextricably bound together in this mass known as humanity. Somewhere, in all the *noes* of life, there is a *yes* to be discovered. It is not just a romantic ideal that obliterates and disguises pain. It is a truly powerful, authoritative and life-giving *yes*.

Out of Billy's death, and oh, how I wanted him to live, emerged a beautiful tapestry of life. I didn't see it at first. Nor did I expect anything positive to surface—I hurt too much. But, through his death I learned truly to value the lives of little children. Through his death I learned to value my children, the healthy children whom I took for granted. Through his death, I learned that the dust will be there tomorrow so go play with my kids today. Through his death I learned how not to be victimized by hospital staff, and others, who tell you what you can or can't do with your life. In a strange sort of way, Billy's death helped give me the courage to get out of a cruel marriage. Through his death, my compassion for others grew. And through his death I discovered this simple prayer that was brought to me on a small medal by one of my Beta Sigma Phi sorority sisters: "God grant me the serenity to accept the things I cannot change, to change the things I can, and the wisdom to know the difference." It has become one of my mainstays.

They were small steps that I took back then in 1971. Baby steps. Since then, each step has brought me closer to a realization of the way in which God works in our lives. That prayer, famous for its use with alcoholics, became my stepping stone to a greater understanding of God's role in my life and my role in prayer.

### Prayer Umbrella

Prayer is something most of us struggle with. Anyone who has ever prayed an "unanswered prayer" knows the frustration—and the disappointment—of feeling that God hasn't heard. Nor does He seem to care about what I feel is deeply significant.

It seems very simplistic to say that God simply answers some of our prayers with a "no." In fact, it sounds as if we're making excuses for God. It sounds like a pat answer to avoid the real question of unanswered prayer. Often it sounds as if we're doing theological gymnastics to protect our faith or the faith of someone we care about.

Plenty has been written on this subject. Pastors will tell us simply that sometimes God says, "No." But, somehow, understanding this concept doesn't seem quite that easy. It's difficult—perhaps because we're so blinded by our own desires. Or, perhaps it's because we still believe that somehow *we* are at the center of the universe instead of God.

A friend once told me that she had given a signed autobiography of a prominent personality to her sister-in-law for Christmas. When the thank-you note came in the mail it read, "Thank you so much for the book. I love reading autobiographies, especially my own." We thought the note back was a hoot. It turned out to be no joke. My friend's sister-in-law had emotional problems that consumed all her thoughts. Behind the humorous nature of this exchange is a tragic sentiment filled with short-sighted, self-consuming thoughts. Yet as obvious a flaw as this is, all of us at some level want others to read our own autobiographies. In our myopic vision and self-centeredness there are times each of us may think our own autobiography is the most important one in the universe.

## Helping Hands

In his book, *Mere Christianity*, C.S. Lewis pointed out that the greatest of sins—and at the very center of sin—is pride. This is our autobiography. Pride is the principal sin that separates us from God. ". . . Pride always means enmity—it *is* enmity. And not only enmity between man and man, but enmity to God." Lewis points out that becoming free from this greatest of all sins is what allows us to enjoy life and to look at God and realize that we don't have to uphold any pretense to be loved and forgiven by Him. One can lose all self-concern and be free to care about others, to consider their thoughts and their feelings. And one is available to help with their needs.

I know that if others hadn't reached out to me when Frank died, my days would have seemed endless. I, in turn, reached out to his ten friends to help them process their grief, then disbelief—their sudden awareness that they weren't the invincible lot they assumed themselves to be.

They learned through each other, themselves and us. We were in it together . . . this healing, grieving process. All of us had our alone times and down times. Mine were filled with self-talk and quiet prayer. And with my own time alone I discovered early on, I wasn't alone. Externally, I felt myself enveloped with a layer of concern—as though someone had literally taken me in their arms. They were loving me, stroking me, telling me I was safe. I was. I now know that I was being lifted and nurtured by God.

If we can lose this self-concern and concentrate on our relationship with God, prayer frees us to begin to know His character. It is only in knowing His character that we can begin to understand that His *noes* are not just theological sidesteppings or excuses, but are instead answers that come from a loving Father who is infinitely concerned for our welfare and well-being. Aren't you grateful for the times He hasn't "answered" your prayers? If God truly gave us everything we asked for, our lives would be a mess. How many women have prayed for a specific man to be their "Mr. Right" only later to be grateful their prayer wasn't answered? How many jobs have we "thought" we wanted and were relieved we didn't get? If God took us with such pedantic literalism that He answered each and every prayer specifically as we prayed—we could only expect utter chaos. Thank God He doesn't.

The question is, then, why does God say "no" to healing a mother with little children from her cancer? Why would God withhold an answer to save my baby from dying? Why would God allow children in Afghanistan to lose arms and legs in a cruel war? Why did God allow six million Jews to be annihilated in the Holocaust? Why did God allow for the blood-letting in Tiananmen Square in the summer of 1989? Why has God said no to me . . . and to you . . . and to others?

## Misconceptions

Part of the problem we encounter is the belief that bad things should happen only to bad people. In his national bestseller, *When Bad Things Happen to Good People,* Harold S. Kushner points out that somewhere deep inside people is the belief that if something bad happens to someone then there must be a reason. One of the first responses we have is, "What did I do to deserve this?" Surely, I could have done nothing so "bad" that the life of my child would be taken.

There's a belief in a direct cause and effect. This is reinforced in our childhood; we are punished for bad behavior and rewarded for good behavior. In the same way, we believe that the things which happen to us here on earth have a direct relationship to our behavior. If we are "good" then God will reward us. If we are "bad" then God will punish us.

That all seems so logical. So down to earth. So full of common sense. But is it? If you are "good," is that a guarantee that everything will go well for you? I don't think so. There are too many people out there whom I have had to work with and around that I would classify as "bad" . . . at times even downright evil. And yet, life's breaks come their way—the decision makers, the people in charge, don't see the bad sides. The "bad" keep getting rewarded. How unjust. How unfair. How like life.

Remember the childhood sidewalk game, "Step on a crack, break your mother's back"? I spent years jumping to different parts of cement—fearing that I would be the cause of my mother eventually breaking her back. This is definitely bad behavior for anyone to inflict on another. Such a silly ditty, yet we all have tapes like these running through our minds. And one of those tapes is that bad things only happen to bad people. Never us. Only them. And good things/blessings happen only to "good" people. Us, you, me—not "them."

The Jews of the Old Testament saw it that way as well. Whenever there was a time of prosperity, *everyone* said, "God is blessing us." If there was a famine, *everyone* said, "God is punishing us." The Book of Job is a classic illustration of this type of mindset.

Job's family died, he lost his fortune and he was stricken with boils. Everyone, including Job's wife, said, "God is doing this to you." Job thought so too. His wife's response was, "Why don't you just curse God and die?" After all, it was God's fault that this disaster was happening to him.

Job's wife wasn't alone in her response. Her reaction was typical in Greek thought as well. In Greek mythology we discover that the common belief was that the gods were up in heaven making it hard for humans on earth. They were sitting around thinking up "divine dirty tricks" that they could play on people. Some of that same philosophy is still around today.

## A Closer Look

But the author of the Book of Job gives us a unique glimpse into the behind-the-scenes events as well as the true nature of God. Job, we discover, is not being punished for his sinfulness. In fact in the very first verse of chapter 1 we're told that he was the most righteous man on the face of the earth. What happened to Job had nothing to do with how "good" or "bad" he was. We're told right up front that what happened to Job was initiated by Satan and allowed by God with one restriction: Satan was not permitted to take Job's life. Admittedly, this presents another problem.

If God is good, and the Bible tells us He is, then why would He allow Job to suffer so? In the Psalms David clearly writes, "For God is good, and he loves goodness" (Psalm 11:7). There must, therefore, be an aspect to the nature of God where He allows things to happen that break His own heart. To say that God gives cancer to a child, that He took Frank from me, that it was His will for Billy to die, would go against the nature of God. Accidents happen. Yes, He allows it. No, He doesn't stop it. Tragedies, bad things that happen to myself and others, break my heart. I suspect, though, they break God's heart more.

God makes it clear that He didn't send His Son into the world to condemn the world. By its very nature, the world was already condemned. It was already messed up by sin, disease, natural disaster, pain and suffering. Instead He said that He came into the world to "seek and to save what was lost" (Luke 19:10 NIV).

If you follow the life of Jesus, He destroyed the myth that God was up in heaven making life hard for His kids. By His example, Jesus showed us that it was His desire to heal us, to cleanse us from our sins, to fix our broken marriages, to ease the pain and suffering in our lives—and ultimately to punish evil.

### Bartering Doesn't Work

To understand God's *noes* we must understand *Him*—His nature. In his book, *Disappointment with God*, Philip Yancey writes on the premise that, ". . . what we think about God and believe about God matters—*really* matters—as much as anything in life matters." He says this, because what we believe about God determines how we live our lives, as illustrated by Cain and Abel, a story that has always fascinated me.

Cain and Abel both knew that God required a specific sacrifice. This was the rule at the time. Abel obeyed while Cain rebelled. Why? I believe it was because Abel knew God's nature. He knew that God was a good and kind and loving Father and so he was obedient. Cain, on the other hand, didn't believe that God was good. He was angry that God didn't accept what *he,* Cain, felt was a good offering.

Often, this is how we are, too. We become angry when God doesn't accept our "good offer:" "If You heal my child, I'll do anything You want; if You get me out of this mess, I promise I'll never do it again." Famous last words. On the basis of our own sincerity, we believe that God should say *"yes."* But for reasons we can't always understand, God says *"no."* He doesn't heal our child; He doesn't get us out of the mess we created. So we become angry. We even retaliate. We retaliate by not going to church, by not praying—why bother? It doesn't work. We retaliate by being less kind to others—kindness and goodness don't pay off.

But anger needs to be directed where it belongs. God doesn't create evil. The Bible says, "The thief's (Satan's) purpose is to steal, kill and destroy. My (God's) purpose is to give life in all its fullness" (John 10:10). Satan is the one who is evil and who taunts us. Of his own free will—which God gave him—Satan became evil, a true advocate of eternal ill-will for all of humanity. But it's not always Satan who causes our problems either. Sometimes it's just the fact that we live in an imperfect world, we're imperfect people, we choose to do evil, we make mistakes, accidents happen.

In *Tough Times Never Last, But Tough People Do!*,
Dr. Robert Schuller penned some very wise words.
"Don't fix the blame, fix the problem." He continues, "If
you've got a problem, don't add to it. Don't make your
problem worse by aggravating it with self-pity, jeal-
ousy, cynicism, hatred, anger, or lack of positive faith
in the future." These are wise words, words that each
of us should try to live by.

When Frank died, I was initially angry with the
situation. God didn't make it happen. It was an accident. It could have been any one of those kids climbing
on the bridge who fell—it just happened to be my
Frank. Did God stop it? No. Could God have prevented
it? Yes. Did it break God's heart? I believe so. But God
chose, because God created this world to be free, not to
intervene. God not only gave us the freedom to be
right, He gave us the freedom to be wrong. And that
freedom extends to all of life, to all of creation. In the
context of that freedom, God chooses at times not to
intervene—yet surprisingly, sometimes God does.
God doesn't always say *no*. Sometimes He says, *not yet.*

One of my friends, Margaret, is a full-time home-
maker with two active kids. Two years ago Margaret
injured her hip, causing her debilitating sciatic nerve
pain. The nature of the injury was so severe and the
pain so intense that she went days and nights without
sleep as she writhed on her bed in agony. Days, weeks
and months went by with no reprieve from the suffering. Her family prayed. Friends in her church prayed.
Nothing happened.

Nothing, that is, for months on end. But slowly,
painfully, step by step, Margaret improved. At times,
the pain was worse than at others. Amazingly, through
it all, she learned to trust God in a way that she never

had before. God's *not yet* was working a far greater good in her life.

Today, my friend will tell you she wishes she had never gone through it. She'll also tell you she's glad she did. Margaret knows and understands the nature of God in a way she never did before. She's still not 100 percent well, but she is much improved. Margaret takes one day at a time—still unable to sit or stand or walk for long periods of time. Today she has hope. What seemed at first to her to be God's *no,* was turning into God's *not yet.* Eventually, she believes that God will fully restore her to her original health. But, getting to that belief, coming to the faith that is her partner today, has been a long, drawn-out and painful process.

On the other hand, God can sometimes surprise us with an unexpected *yes.* One of my colleagues, Jean, had earned an excellent reputation in the media field. Jean agonized over the tyranny that her co-employees were daily placed under. Unreasonable demands of time and energy were the norm, not the exception. The unfairness of the demands became an internal cause for prayer—and eventually a source of Jean's release.

When she was in her element in the media field, strategizing her next marketing ploy—she could ignore the surrounding chaos. That is until one Thursday morning. With no forewarning she was laid off. She didn't want to leave her job. She loved it. She didn't like the management style but she liked the people she was working with. But suddenly, without even the standard warnings, she was set adrift. Instead of answering her prayer in the way she expected—making the situation better—God removed her from the situation. God said an unexpected *yes*—*but not in the format requested.* That *yes* turned out to be one of the best things that ever happened to my friend. Her health improved, her finances turned around and today she'll tell you that she's enjoying life at a higher level than she's ever experienced before.

We live in a complex world filled with wars and pressure and unfairness. Somewhere in the tyranny of this life, there is a refuge that we can find in a good, loving and kind God. There is a principle I've learned over the years: If you blame God as the source of your problems, you cut off the source of your help. In the midst of your problems, in the midst of not understanding, if you turn to Him, He'll comfort you and give you the peace He promised: "The peace of God which passes *all* understanding." He may answer, "*yes*," He may answer, "*not yet*," or He may answer, "*no*." But one thing is certain. If you nourish a *no* it will lead you *nowhere*. . . .

# 3

# Nourishing a *No* Leads to Nowhere

Never in my life had I gotten stuck like this. This time, I was stuck. Really stuck. And it wasn't just in a small way. I was so lost, I couldn't even make a phone call. At least, after Frank's death, I was able to go through the mechanics. Certain rituals were expected of me. A service had to be planned. As soon as morning dawned, I had begun making calls to all the various people involved. I called Frank's place of work, I tracked down in-laws, I phoned our friends to tell them that John's birthday dinner had to be cancelled. All those calls were painful. All those questions that my calls generated compounded our hurts, pains and fears.

But this time, I was paralyzed. For someone on the outside looking in, being misled and cheated in a business venture may seem trivial in comparison to the loss of my two children, but somehow, this was my catastrophic event—my breaking point.

In living color, my work, a creative project that I had spent years developing, was being destroyed before my very eyes. Another child was dying. Worse yet, I couldn't believe that the death blows were delivered by someone I had trusted, respected, even defended. It was more than I could bear.

I had been lied to by representatives of the company. I believed that contracts had been altered after my signature had been obtained. Promised reimbursements of expenses amounting to many thousands of dollars were brushed aside. To me, everything was done to destroy my project—my baby. The personal devastation was so total that I couldn't make a simple phone call, I couldn't work, I didn't think I could even live. I was paralyzed. I was a mess.

As a professional speaker in the public eye, I had learned to develop a great facade—to pretend when things weren't going well. There was never the luxury of shutting down. The show must go on! This time, though, it was different. I panicked. I had enormous financial obligations and every penny of the money due from the grant had been budgeted, planned for—and a great deal of it already spent. When my work and my efforts were sabotaged, one of my "babies" was being harmed, and my very being cried out in pain.

My legal counsel assured me that my case was strong. The evidence appeared to be clearly in my favor. But was it? How can you measure years of work outside of the hard dollars spent? I was convinced that I was legally right, but . . . . My years of experience in the business world have shown me that just about anyone can be right in a legal situation, and still lose—that, in fact, the attorneys became the overall winners in the end. For some, legalese becomes the solution. For me, it wasn't.

When your internal dialogue has built up, it becomes a mountain, and I couldn't quite get by that mountain. You see, the real issue was, I just couldn't take a third death. Weren't two children enough? I had carried that project not just for nine months, but for several years. I had lived with it, defended it, supported it, nurtured it and given birth to it—just to have it snatched away from me.

## Not Another No

I couldn't face another *no.* This time I broke. Openly broke. For the first time in my life there was no fight left in me. There were no inner reservoirs of strength. No *yeses* behind the unexplained no. I was stuck in that gray, mournful area of the *no that leads to nowhere.* I had entered what I now term the "being stuck syndrome." And I couldn't get out by myself.

Desperate, I needed help. I got down on my knees begging God to end my pain, my hurt, the betrayal I felt so deeply. I couldn't talk to anyone close to me without tears in my eyes. After all I had gone through, for the first time I felt life was not worth living—I was ready to throw in the towel. Give up. Check out.

I called my friend and former pastor, John Snyder. We all need a John Snyder in our lives and I was grateful for mine. I couldn't talk without tears. Patiently he listened. Then he spoke words that I'll always be grateful for. He didn't tell me to "buck up." He didn't ask me just to forget it and move on. He listened, then he expressed his own outrage: "This really makes me angry." Oh, how I needed that! It made him mad too! He saw the injustice. There was no attempted cover-up, no "Christian blackmail" telling me my feelings were invalid and if I were truly the person I should be I would feel forgiveness toward the malicious perpetrator of the crime. It was okay to cry. It was okay to be human. It was okay to feel lost and hopeless and despairing of life itself. He helped me to process my feelings internally. I had a partner in pain, who was there for me to spill it out.

John Snyder was the first step. The second was a little harder for me. I had always been so independent. So self-assured. So . . . together. At least, that's what everyone always thought. This time the "I can do it myself syndrome" broke. I couldn't do it by myself. I couldn't do anything for myself, much less anyone else. I had to reach out to friends. To family. That was a big step for me. Everyone had always counted on me, the pillar. And you know what? They were there.

### Reaching Out

When I called, I asked for their thoughts, their strategies, most of all, I asked for their prayers. Help came freely—with love and concern. "How much money do you need to get over the hurdle?" asked Carol as we sat down to a glass of iced tea. Carol had been my business partner before we had parted ways.

My friend Marilyn called to say hello—did she get an earful! The following day a check for $1,000 was delivered to my home with a note, "I love you! I know that God has plans for you." That note, that check, broke me out. I am loved, I am a valuable person. Another person cares for me. Marilyn and other friends, Coreen, Joyce and Nicole routinely checked in with me—reminding me that I was loved, my voice was important—that they kept me uppermost in their prayers.

One Saturday I poured out my heart to a group of speakers within The National Speakers Association of Northern California called, "The Masters." They were stunned. This was show and tell time—this was when we got to brag, to share good news from one previous month. Everyone in the group was always doing great. We were the ones on the top. Successful. We were the ones on stage. Our stories were always terrific. We always looked great. We made money—some of us, a lot. "What do you mean you have 'garbage' going on in your life?" Yet here I was, immersed in a giant trash heap. The sharp business woman had been shafted. Really shafted.

After that Saturday, several notes came in from some of the speakers in the group thanking me for opening up. I had reminded them that life's not always a merry-go-round. In getting out of the "being stuck syndrome" I had been forced to reach out. And in reaching out, I touched other lives. Sharing my hurt gave permission for others to admit that sometimes all was not great. Their caring, their friendship and their prayers became my food. I was beginning to take in the nutrition I needed.

As long as I had been wallowing in my anger, my rage at being taken, I was stuck. Going nowhere. But when I began to look outward, to reach out my hand to others, something magical, mystical, began to happen —that special something that happens when one life touches yours and your life touches another. I was no longer fighting a private war. I had friends and allies to see me through.

### Forward . . . Looking Back

What my friends reminded me of were my accomplishments. I was so devastated, so broken, so bereft of self-esteem, that I had forgotten what I *had* done. Here I had spent several years on what I thought was one of my best creative projects to date—and my confidence had been shattered via the nonsupport of a group I trusted.

Ironically, as I was experiencing this tremendous pain, I was committed to write a book on confidence for MasterMedia, a publisher for whom I had written a book the previous year. Crazy, here I was doing a survey on confidence, writing a book on confidence . . . and I lacked it! What a sense of humor God has—or was it something else? Would this something add strength to the surgery on my life that I was experiencing?

Out of the hundreds of women interviewed and thousands surveyed for the book, *The Confidence Factor*, one of the commandments that surfaced was this: take credit for your accomplishments. I had forgotten that I had any. In fact, I had quite a list of them. Here I was, full sighted, yet totally blind to my own value, my own worth.

My friends and family helped me get back on the road of taking credit for what I had done. It was their support that held me up during my time of need. And through it I was able to realize that the world hadn't come to an end. This was the beginning—a starting over, so to speak—of my next phase of growth.

What developed out of this was a lot of dialogue in prayer. In one sense, prayer didn't change anything. It didn't make the world more just. It didn't cause the grant agent to see the wrongdoing and come crawling to me begging for forgiveness. It didn't even change the financial notes that were due . . . and now very overdue. What did change was *me*.

Prayer was the vehicle that took me down a new road, a road of peace. It was a road of trusting that in this messed-up world there's Someone out there who cares about me. Someone hears me and understands me more than anyone else. And Someone can comfort me and best of all—surprise me!

Poet Ralph Waldo Emerson wrote, "When it is dark enough, men see the stars." My eyes weren't open in the right direction, yet in my blackest night, there were stars out there waiting for me. And there are stars out there waiting for you as well.

### Heroes Speak

Winston Churchill was called on to give an address at Harrow School in October of 1941. The press set up their cameras. They were ready with huge rolls of film to record every word of wisdom spoken by this great leader. Reporters had come with pencils in hand and notebooks ready to capture the lengthy words that were sure to follow. Anticipation mounted as Churchill stepped to the podium. But rather than giving an extensive treatise, Churchill spoke only twenty-nine words. Contained in those words was his formula for victory: "*Never* give in, never give in, never, never, never, never —in nothing, great or small, large or petty—never give in except to convictions of honor and good sense." And then he sat down. End of speech. His audience was stunned and then burst into thundering applause.

In the face of advancing Nazi troops, Churchill stood by this formula. Defeat was not an option. Evil could not triumph. He would not—*could not*—give up. History records the victory won by his indomitable spirit, and the spirit of so many who bravely fought beside him.

Those are yesteryear's heroes. Dead. Gone. What about today's? The heroes who are alive . . . breathing? We are surrounded by them. Heroes come in all kinds of shapes, sizes, sexes. You know several. Possibly, one is you.

As an author and professional speaker, I have the opportunity to meet many unique people—people I would not have had the opportunity to meet unless I was speaking somewhere in a small town or a big city. Your town.

My heroes tend to be living people—I don't know them all personally. But I do know that there is someone I know who knows someone else. And they can make a connection if I really want it to happen. After all, having heroes, men and women whom you admire for their strength, their vision, their spunk, doesn't necessarily mean that you have to be close friends with them.

I am blessed with many men and women who are heroes—men and women who make me reach, aspire higher. Heroes like Sharon Komlos, who drove home from work one afternoon and in a flash was blinded by a gunshot wound, assaulted, raped and slashed. And yet, she says that her faith is her mainstay. God has been with her and today, almost ten years since her "incident," she says that her life is great. Sharon Komlos inspires me.

Heroes like W. Mitchell, who was severely burned in an accident that fused the nubs of his fingers. Now kids in school yards call him "monster"; he went on to learn to pilot a plane, crashed and was paralyzed. Before the second accident, he claims that there were 10,000 things he could do, now there are 9,000. He can either dwell on the 1,000 he lost, or focus on the 9,000 he has left. The W in his name stands for *Wonderful.* W. Mitchell inspires me.

Heroes like Nicole Schapiro, who was raised in a silent convent for eight years during World War II before her mother was able to track her down and reclaim her, who was a revolutionary in the Hungarian Revolution, who negotiated herself out of a firing line, who convinced the about-to-be President Dwight Eisenhower to allow her and other Hungarians to immigrate to the United States versus the originally intended New Zealand, who arrived in America with $10 and lived on the streets of New York for six months as a bag lady, who educated herself, eventually earning a master's degree and becoming the first woman vice president with a major bank.

Heroes like Captain Gerald Coffee, who was a POW in Vietnam for seven years, surviving and being a key factor in the survival of so many of his fellow men who were imprisoned during his time there. I am in awe when he demonstrates his "Tap Code," the linkage that bonded the men from cell to cell. Their ability to expand their educations by tapping out foreign languages, sciences, literature—each man sharing his area of expertise with the others—thrills me. Each evening, they would sign off, "God bless," to each other. Captain Gerald Coffee inspires me.

Today, Nicole Schapiro is a motivational and inspirational speaker and consultant who specializes in team building and negotiating. Clearly she, as Captain Gerald Coffee has, have carried and translated her intense wartime experiences, experiences that few of us today can closely relate to, to the general public. Although Nicole Schapiro is not a Christian, she is a woman who was cared for and supported by Christians during the war. Her story, the inspiration that she gives to audiences around the world, is awesome. Nicole Schapiro is one of my close friends, one of my heroes. She leaves rubber bands with her audiences . . . a continual reminder to them to stretch, especially when times look bleak.

When I mention Joan Rivers as a hero, many raise their eyebrows. But think about it. She was publicly fired with millions watching it on TV, more millions reading about it in the press. This event was followed by the tragic death of her husband of many years. Her pain was immense, yet she stayed in the public eye, confronted her critics, and took her lumps. Big ones. Then she started a new show. Her strength to continue has created hope for many. Joan Rivers and her tenacity inspire me.

Everyone has his own battlefields. Whether they are like those Captain Coffee confronted in Vietnam, the tragedy of a gas tank exploding as W. Mitchell experienced, the public humiliation that Joan Rivers faced, the loss of a critical sense (vision) that Sharon Komlos once took for granted, the separation of family that Nicole experienced—all are battlefields. Some have major skirmishes, others minor.

Today, we still live in a battlefield—a different kind of battlefield. But nevertheless, it's still a war. The lines are drawn. Will we be defeated by the *noes* that will inevitably come along in life? Or will we, like Churchill, look the enemy squarely in the eye, with a glint of determination, and say along with him, "I'll *never* give in!"

The apostle Paul's voice is heard throughout the New Testament. He says it with a twist. Who knew better than Paul what it was like to suffer hardship? He had been stoned, imprisoned, shipwrecked, bitten by a poisonous snake, persecuted on every side. Yet listen to his words: "It is God himself, in his mercy, who has given us this wonderful work [of telling his Good News to others], and so *we never give up. . . .* We are pressed on every side by troubles, but not crushed and broken. We are perplexed because we don't know why things happen as they do, but we don't give up and quit. We are hunted down, but God never abandons us. We get knocked down, but we get up again and keep going" (2 Corinthians 4:1, 8, 9).

Paul, like Churchill and Coffee and Mitchell and Komlos, and Schapiro and Rivers, knew that to give up was not an option. They each had an inner drive, an inner strength of conviction, that spurred them on to greatness in the face of extreme obstacles.

The nobility of Churchill's cause was brought about because the evil forces of a wicked Nazi regime, led by a madman, had intruded its way into the fiber of history. Churchill might have preferred to be a lesser known leader in peaceful times rather than to have had to conquer the insidious, venomous poison let loose by a perverted political power. His greatness is measured in part by the contrast seen around him. Even so, he never became stuck in his *"no."* He didn't get sidetracked by stopping at the *"whys"* of Nazism. He moved beyond the obstacles with great determination and strength. And he won.

President John F. Kennedy is often credited with George Bernard Shaw's penned immortal words, "You see things; and you ask, 'Why?' But I dream things that never were; and I say, 'Why not?'"

Why not? Dream big! See beyond the death—beyond the pain, beyond despair, beyond hopelessness—and dream of things that never were. Doing this won't answer all your whys. It most definitely can't change the past. But dreaming big, reaching beyond, can and will change the future if you don't get stuck in your *no*.

Contained within each one of us is the potential for greatness. Not necessarily prominence. Not necessarily greatness and success as defined by money or materialism or status. But true greatness. Moral greatness. Life-changing greatness.

You may never be a politician. You may never be in the public eye. You may never stand before kings or princes or heads of state. You may never change the course of history. You may never pilot a plane, be in a POW camp, be blinded, be separated from your family or fired on TV. But you can change the course of your life and the lives of those around you. You can change *your* world. You *can* make a difference. In your home, in your community. You can take the *noes* of your life and crush them under your feet and stand firmly planted on the *yeses* of tomorrow.

# 4

# Yeses Are
# Not Instant

■　　　　■　　　　■

Never, never, never—in a million years—never did I think this would happen to me. I grew up watching television shows like "Father Knows Best," "Leave it to Beaver," and "Perry Mason." In these make-believe worlds, families worked together to solve their problems. Husbands loved and cherished their wives and their perfect children. They lived in an arena where dreams came true, where fairy tales really happened. These shows always said truth outweighed dishonesty. In "Perry Mason," the falsely accused always got their lives back in order the last ten minutes of the show.

When I married Steve, I knew that all of it, all the dreams, all the hopes, all the fairy tales were true. But several years later, as I came tumbling down two flights of stairs—pushed down in a violent fit of rage by my husband—my dreams were shattered for the last time. All hope of happiness cracked with each thud of my body. Bloodied and bruised, beaten down emotionally and physically, I knew I had reached the end. That was the last time he would lay a hand on me.

Still smarting with the pain of my battered body—and the pain of Billy's recent death—I made my decision. This was it. I didn't care how ugly Steve thought my nose and face were. I didn't care how stupid he thought I was. I didn't care how low he had made me feel. Deep down inside I knew that no matter what kind of terrible person he had convinced me I was, I wasn't terrible or stupid or ugly enough to deserve this.

Somehow Billy's death had changed me. When I finally realized that I wasn't required to be victimized by anyone or anything—be it hospital staff or husband —I knew I was free to begin taking steps to change my circumstances. Rearrange my life.

A job offer from a friend became the open door to my escape. He had wanted to help me get over my grief from Billy's death. It helped. But it also helped pave the way for my freedom. Plans began to formulate in my mind. Finally, after consulting a lawyer, I told Steve I wanted a divorce and I asked him to leave.

Steve left. But he too consulted a lawyer and within days he had moved back. My plans began to backfire. He would seek sole custody of our three children.

One thing I hadn't anticipated was dishonesty. All the rules of fair play were thrown out the window as the battle began. Tragically, as happens all too often, the children were at the heart of the battle. All along I was certain that I would attain custody—after all, I was their mother, their primary caregiver. It would just be a matter of time. Yet, unbelievably, incredibly, in spite of their father's mean streaks, in spite of his vile temper, in spite of his drinking problems, in spite of his nonparticipation as a parent, he gained custody of our three children. Money won. My belief in "Perry Mason" was shattered.

### Enough's Enough

It wasn't enough that Billy had died. It wasn't enough that I had been brutalized and beaten. It wasn't enough that I had been slandered in court.

It wasn't enough that I had been victimized by lying and cheating. It wasn't enough that my family didn't support my decision to divorce my ex-husband. Now, as if all that weren't enough, I had to suffer the loss of my three kids. It just wasn't fair! The resounding answer was no with a capital N. Once again, I was the unwilling victim in a life filled with brick walls with the letters N-O hung firmly at the center.

Surprisingly, life didn't end. I thought it would. Throughout the trial I had been harassed at work—my boss and manager were even threatened. Although they knew it wasn't my fault, I was eventually fired from my job as a stockbroker's assistant. They didn't think I could concentrate on my work. The time was 1972.

Just before I lost my job I was notified that my car insurance had been cancelled. My husband had done it—and according to California law at that time, he had the right to do this and just about anything else he wanted to do. And he did. He not only cancelled my car insurance, he kept the refund on the premium. The agent told me that since I was going through a divorce, I was unstable. Unstable?! I was the most "stable" I had ever been.

Steve also cancelled the credit cards that I had obtained in my own name using my own credit from my own job. Gifts that had been given to both of us were transferred to his name. He did just about everything he could to wipe me out—including robbing me of the children. I was attacked on all fronts—mentally, physically and financially. None of my friends could understand how this could have happened. Not one. I certainly couldn't—why would they?

Everything was going wrong. I decided that

Southern California was too small for the two of us, and I looked for work away from my pain center. After several interviews, I decided to accept a position as a stockbroker with E. F. Hutton in Northern California. I tried to pretend the pain wasn't there by anesthetizing it with twelve- to fourteen-hour days. How could this have happened? I could hardly face the reality of it. Days blurred into weeks, weeks into months.

After the divorce and losing my kids, I learned that people lied, cheated and stole. All with no evident remorse. This went on for one and a half years, one and a half lonely years. I knew the heartache of not having my kids with me full time. Every weekend I could, I either flew them up to visit or flew down to see them. It was awful.

Steve played games—the kids would be sick when he sent them up. He wouldn't be at his home when I took them back, causing me to miss my return flight home. The game was just about up. Steve had "won" the kids through gifts and promises, but the promises were gone. All the "good" times were bygones. His ploy had been to get me back by withholding Shelley, Frank and Sheryl. When he realized I wasn't coming back, the game was over. He remarried a few weeks after our divorce was final.

Looking back I can now see that there was a *yes* smack dab in the middle of all that mess. The *yes* I got was that I had enough alone time to become my own person—a real person. For the first time in my life, I was beginning to discover who I was meant to be. I was able to reach out, to stretch my abilities. I discovered new avenues of expression. And I realized that I had a purpose in life to fulfill, a path to follow, which was mine and mine alone.

## Patience . . . A Must

This didn't happen overnight. This was by no means instantaneous—and by no means easy. The process of becoming a whole person took over a year and a half—perhaps the longest year and a half of my life. I had to wait for my *yes*. Not just for it to happen, but also to realize that there even was a *yes* to uncover in the midst of this horrible situation.

Part of one process included meeting John after vowing that the "dating scene" was not my cup of tea. The rules had changed significantly from the early sixties. The year 1973 was a different game. I wanted nothing to do with men. I didn't trust them. Returning a borrowed book to a friend, I met John one afternoon. He later invited me for dinner and actually did the dishes. Was I impressed! He teamed with me to coach girls' soccer. A year later, we married with the soccer team giving us a send-off party!

Little did I know there was yet another long-awaited *yes* lurking behind the ugliness of the divorce. Ironically, it happened at Easter time—the time when death makes way for life. Out of the death and destruction of my divorce, something new was getting ready to spring to life. The kids were up for spring vacation when the phone rang. I didn't recognize the voice on the line. I was immediately wary, unsure of what was wrong. The voice was the children's father. He asked if I would do an old friend a favor—would I keep the kids for another week? He and Vicki were having problems. Would I? Not only did I assure him I would keep the kids another week, I also told him they weren't coming back. Check and checkmate. A year later, formal custody was reversed with the same judge sitting on the bench. He kept muttering, "How did this happen?"—money, power, lies, that's how. My vindication had come at last. But more importantly, my children were back and doing well in school.

A long and painful *no* had unfolded to reveal three very important *yeses* in my life. Having my children gone had "bought" me my first *yes*. It bought me the freedom and independence I had needed to pull my own life together. Another *yes* was having John come into my life—a kind, gentle and loving man. And in due time, when the healing process had been given enough time, my children were back. Home. My long-awaited *yes*.

Looking back, the time I was alone allowed me to get established in my career, paving the way for being able to support my kids financially. And I joined the ranks of millions of divorced mothers—the judge awarded child support but we never saw it. I had been given the tools to take care of my kids, and I was thankful that I could support them.

If I had been in control, if I had been God, and if things had been done my way, I wouldn't have made me wait for any of my *yeses*. Nor would I have had experienced the pain of the past. My mind plays "what if" games at times—as most of us do. What if? If only. In some of my worse times, I have done my "what if" as in, what if I were God—how would I make the world be?

If that "what if" were thrown to you, you would probably decide that everyone should have a perfect life. That there would be peace around the world. That no one would ever suffer through the disfigurement of a fire, or accident, or birth, the loss of a child, or a loved one, the terror of a rapist, the destruction of nature—if you were God. Nor would you make anyone wait to find a *yes* behind their *no*.

But for some reason, waiting seems to be part of the *yes* process. You've heard the saying, "Good things come to those who wait." Good ideas take time to germinate. Babies take time to grow in the womb. Crops take time to mature before the harvest. Rarely does anything happen overnight.

By nature, we humans are impatient. Today's environment seems to make us more so. The Plastic/Now Society wants it all. Better yet, they want it yesterday; scratch the tomorrows. When pain, hurt, tragedy or loss are experienced, an instant Band-Aid is demanded—one that will clot and seal immediately. The Plastic/Now Society is used to the programming of modern television—a commercial break every seven minutes or so. Just enough time to take a breather, to get refreshment, to escape from the dramas or tensions of life.

Well, life is not a video or a show on the big screen. Life rarely gives a commercial break, and certainly they do not come every seven minutes. To be successful in the art of life, the art of patience must be practiced. Moses experienced generations of elapsed time between the genesis of a mission and the actual Exodus. And yet, he had to be prepared. Never knowing that any breaks would come, he waited on the backside of a desert. Moses even tried to get out of it all, but God said *no*—then He made Moses wait. And wait. And wait. God's *no* to Moses, then His long awaited *yes*—all served to bring about the emancipation of an entire nation. During his waiting period, Moses was learning and growing and preparing to become a leader of great strength and perseverance. It was no short process.

Forty years elapsed. No one, especially God, was in any great hurry.

One of my newer friends is Morris Goodman. In a matter of a few minutes, his life was changed forever. As he was piloting his small plane, the engine sputtered over the landing field, trapping him in a mass of metal as it hurtled toward the ground. The crash left him with a broken neck and a body so badly mangled that he wasn't expected to live. Unbelievably, he did.

Unable to speak, eat, move or breathe without the use of a respirator, Morris was determined to regain the full use of his body. Thousands prayed for him, but the doctors said his goal was impossible. Yet a year later, he was walking in his home.

Just before the anniversary of his accident, a large gathering of his insurance colleagues asked Morris to give the invocation at their annual meeting. He thanked them for their love, support and prayers the past year and he closed the invocation with, ". . . if I have just one prayer answered, it is that You be as good to everyone here today during the coming year as You have been to me over the past year. Amen."

Today, Morris Goodman speaks on motivation and courage to groups worldwide and is the author of *The Miracle Man*. Pain is his constant companion. His accident sold himself on life—when his engine failed, his fate was out of his hands. When he regained consciousness, he had a choice—wait to die or live his life as it presently is to the fullest. Morris Goodman's faith, his belief in God as a partner was expanded when he came to the point in his life that loving God was more important than trying to understand all the suffering he had been through.

## Overriding the Negatives

If you will keep your vision open, another purpose will come forth. Something far greater—far more valuable. Something that goes beyond your own limited sphere of life.

This was true in the case of Joseph in the Old Testament. His older brothers sold him down the highway. Joseph suffered incredibly, for no reason, other than his brothers' envy of him. He hadn't committed any crime other than childish arrogance. It was in the prison and in the palace of another that he grew up and matured. He became a man of great stature and vision. These were long, painful years. They were years of deprivation in a crude, miserable jail cell, years of separation from his family. Only in retrospect can we see so clearly that the *yes* of God was being worked out in an intricate plan to save Joseph's family from the coming famine. He was part of a larger plan. Through Joseph's words is discovered an incredible insight: "As far as I am concerned, God turned into good what you meant for evil, for he brought me to this high position I have today so that I could save the lives of many people" (Genesis 50:20).

Could it be that God takes the evil things of this world, the tragedies, the accidents, the violence, the insidious crimes committed against others and somehow, miraculously, turns them around to good?

Difficult as it may be to understand, there is a promise that God gives us: "And we know that all happens to us is working for our good if we love God and are fitting into his plans" (Romans 8:28). God Himself promises that when we look to Him in our circumstances, no matter how painful, how difficult, how unbearable or how impossible they might be, that somewhere, somehow, He will turn it to good. He will redeem it. Sounds impossible, but with God I have learned that nothing, absolutely nothing, is impossible.

To understand God's plan, to understand the *yes* behind the *no*, a step must be taken. The brewing turmoil of the past must be left behind—a move must be made into the future. The time must come when you begin to move on with assurance into the *yeses* of tomorrow. How long do we have to wait for this to happen? As long as it takes.

# 5

# From Treading in Turmoil to Moving On with Assurance

■ ■ ■

After Frank's accident, I felt that I had experienced seven years of agony in seven weeks. Words can't begin to express the grief and torment as we awaited news of finding his body. My anguish was heightened by a recurring nightmare—seeing Frank's body swooshing around . . . around . . . around. I assumed it would be found within a few days of the accident. I had assumed wrong.

With my recurring nightmare, I called one of my friends, a psychologist. She suggested that I try and block it, to stop thinking that way—it could actually be happening, or my mind could be a partner in creating the swooshing that I kept seeing.

Still, the nightmare continued. My sister-in-law, Mary, called to see how we were doing. She heard my anguish and suggested that the body might have gone out to sea. I then decided to speak to the coroner, someone I thought would be experienced in this area. With the time of night, the tides, the currents and the weather, he assured me that most likely, the body had gone out to sea.

Since Frank loved to fish and had been doing so since he was a little squirt, I decided that this was a fitting exit for him. Frank was laid to rest in my mind in the sea—a place he loved to go. My favorite photo is of two-year-old Frank holding up his first trout. My nightmares stopped.

Even so, inside I wasn't doing well—in fact I was doing horribly. Everyone thought things were fine, but I continued to deteriorate. Frank's friends needed some kind of closure, too. The day after his memorial service, several of them picked me up and drove John, Sheryl, Shelley and their aunt Maureen up on top of a hill. There they mounted a street sign, *Frank's Lane,* "borrowed" from Menlo Park, our home town at the time. I later called City Hall which assured me that the sign was now a gift—better in the redwoods than in a college dorm! Assuming it would only be a matter of days, I promised to scatter Frank's ashes up there.

Later that week, we had asked all of Frank's friends up to our house and invited them to take whatever items of Frank's they wanted—bikes, skis, boots, shoes, tools, clothes—anything and everything. Frank was part of their lives, too. If there was anything they wanted, we wanted them to have something to add to their memories. Today, fourteen years later, it still pleases me when one of the gang reminds me that he has some item Frank loved.

### Expect the Unexpected

I had underestimated. Surely they would find his body. Seven weeks later I came home from school with two of my classmates and there was a message from my father to call. I returned the call and he proceeded to tell me that a reporter from a neighboring city had tracked him down. Frank's body had surfaced. I was stunned.

We had moved three months before his death. For some reason, the Coast Guard couldn't track any reported missing people, and the ID that Frank had on him included his driver's license and social security number, but the address was different from where we currently lived. No one could find us, that is until twelve hours after his body had been located by a duck hunter. The people who had bought our house couldn't remember where we moved, so the reporter started tracking and found my father's phone number in Los Angeles, 450 miles away.

My father started off the call, "You know it has been something that we all have been expecting." I didn't know what he was going to say—I anticipated that he was going to tell me that my mother had died. She had been sick for years. I had already mentally set myself up to support him. Instead, he proceeded to tell me that Frank's body had been found. It had surfaced and a reporter was trying to track me down. I felt that I had been thrown a curve ball, from an area totally unexpected.

The visions I had been having had come true—Frank washing around in the marsh water. All his buddies were relieved—they could get closure, have his body finally resting up at *Frank's Lane*. For me, it was death all over again. I sank deeper into depression, barely functional—spiraling downward.

I called the reporter, who filled in the missing information, at least all that he knew. It felt like a three-ring circus. I also felt that no one seemed to know who was on first base. Records were missing. The state didn't show anything. The Coast Guard showed nothing. And the police had nothing.

The reporter had tracked down a news story in my local paper. Working backward, he eventually found my father in Los Angeles. The other paper hadn't originally covered the story, although the reporter couldn't figure that out—it had been the lead news item over Labor Day on stations surrounding the Bay Area of Northern California. A law suit had been filed against the state because of the dangers the bridge posed. The reporter became my ally in my quest to put pressure on the state. Stories popped up in other papers, putting immense pressure on the state finally to do something about the bridge—to fix it once and for all.

After a series of bureaucratic hassles, I was allowed to claim Frank's body and have it cremated. My daughter Shelley and I went down to pick up his ashes —a simple task, or so we thought. Instead, they were lost. It took the caretaker over an hour to find them. Meanwhile, as we sat in the office, the two security guards were like zombies, glued to the TV, watching a movie. An older couple was arguing between themselves—and with the mortician on duty—about what to do with their bodies when they died. Shelley and I just sat, taking in the entire scene—it was crazy, zany, bizarre. Shelley leaned over and quipped, "Frank would have loved this." It made me laugh out loud—he would have!

Finally the missing ashes were found. They were delivered to me in a brown, wrapped cardboard box. It made noises inside—a surprise. It rattled. Little did I suspect that there would be pieces of bone, not pure ashes to ashes as I had thought it would be.

I took the ashes home and put the box away in an old redwood chest in Frank's room, knowing that they needed to be scattered so that he could finish his journey. For me to do that, I felt I had to wait for all his friends to come home. That wouldn't be until Christmas time when everyone would be back for the holidays from schools and jobs.

## The Final Gathering

Christmas time brought horrible storms. There were black, angry clouds—as black as I have ever seen them. It reminded me of the darkness that fell when Jesus spoke the words on the cross, "It is finished." Deathly black.

Twenty-five of us trekked up the hillside—the storms held off. I had transferred Frank's ashes to a large casserole dish—his favorite. He had loved macaroni and cheese and it seemed appropriate that this dish be part of his transition to his final resting place. At the top of the hill, it dawned on me that I had left the dish with the ashes behind on the kitchen table. Down his best friend Kit and I came—after all, Frank was the guest of honor. There was no doubt in my mind that Frank would have been amused. Somehow, forgetting the bowl, getting caught up with all the kids we hadn't seen for three months, was typical for our house.

All of us shared our thoughts, our hopes, our dreams, our fears. We planted a redwood tree at *Frank's Lane*, a tree that did best in a "community" type of setting with other redwoods—just as human beings do. I read a poem Frank's grandmother had sent:

> God's love is like a fortress
> and we seek protection there.
> When the waves of tribulation
> seem to drown us in despair.

God's love is like a harbor
where our souls can find sweet rest
from the struggles and the tension
of life's fast and futile quest.

God's love is like a beacon
burning bright with faith and prayer.
And through the changing scenes of life,
we can find a haven there.

*Author Unknown*

We burned it and dropped it into the hole where the tree roots would go. We gathered around. Kit held the bowl and I began to scatter the ashes in a circle by their feet. Each friend took a handful of Frank's ashes and scattered them into the wind that afternoon—a powerful closure and their final goodbye to their friend.

Within minutes after we came back down the hill, the storm broke and it rained and rained and rained. Somehow it seemed appropriate. The dark storm of my life was passing. The time for rain had arrived. And soon, after the rains, life would spring forth. New life out of the ashes of my winter months of Frank's death. I had been treading in turmoil long enough—long enough to begin the healing process. Long enough to find the beginnings of closure. Now, at last, I could begin to move on with assurance and rebuild on the remaining foundation of my life.

If given a choice, none of us would choose suffering. None would choose the pain of death, of failure, of illness, of life's never-ending problems. Yet each person who has survived has grown significantly—has experienced a vision that he or she wouldn't have had without the suffering.

At the opening of this book I wrote of how Frank's death changed my life. Frank lives on in a profound way, for he not only touched my life, he has touched the lives of thousands of people that he never knew. Always—when I speak publicly—Frank is part of my presentation, the agonies and ecstasies of being a parent and the three gifts that he gave me: the renewal of my spirituality, the "little kid spirit" and re-looking at who and what I was and where I was going. Each time I share, people come up to me afterwards, touched by Frank's three gifts, and enriched in their own lives.

## The Badge of Courage

Jane Handly is a friend who has experienced great joy—and great pain—in her life. To look at her you would never guess. She is one of my speaker cronies, a woman who has made the difference in so many lives —whether it's a motivational talk for overcoming adversity or on customer service, her specialty.

When Jane was four, rain had dampened the day, so her mother had an idea. She would boil some eggs and the two children could color them—and best of all, eat them when they finished! At the age of four, Jane thought that was great fun. She finished her first egg in just two minutes. Jane begged her mother for the next egg. Her mother was busy talking to a neighbor and told her to wait a moment. In her childish zeal, Jane pulled over a stool, climbed upon it, reached into the boiling water, and when pulling her hand out, fell off the stool pulling the entire pot of scalding water on herself. Jane was severely burned. While in the hospital, her teeth decayed and fell out and her head was shaved to cut down on the chance of infection. She was expected to die. Miraculously, she lived. What remained were horrible physical scars.

Children mocked her odd appearance. They called her "monster." All the while, her mother was at her side, telling her that beauty is on the inside. If the kids were going to call her monster, then she should be the best monster she could be!

Remarkably, Jane went on to win a beauty contest. But not before she had suffered more. At ten, she had a bout with cancer. As an adult, she experienced the heartbreak of divorce. Yet her indomitable spirit is truly inspiring.

Not too long ago, I interviewed her for another book I was writing, *The Confidence Factor*. Jane's words have stuck with me:

> When we think about being alive versus just being, it makes life an adventure and then there's a rapture for being alive. It's a different emotion. Nourish your imagination, love your imperfections, every wrinkle, every long toe, every crooked tooth, just love them and bless them because they're yours and they're unique and they're wonderful. For me, I look in the mirror and I see one good breast and one that I got at a fire sale. And I love my scars *because they represent my healing.*

Can you imagine that? She loves her scars! Whether it's a childhood trauma, a physical disability, a tragic accident—these are the very things that cause us to search for answers, that drive us to find relief. Wounds are the vehicles for healing, for the understanding that can be gained. Wounds turn out to be motivational. And the scars they leave behind, visible and invisible, are the healing each of us processes through.

## The One and Only

Your scars make you uniquely you. They are the reminders that we live in a human world of imperfection—a world where so many others are hurting and needing the kind of comfort that only you—in your uniqueness—can give. That encourages me.

Surely there are many others who can talk about God's *noes*. But only I can share with you the healing process that I went through after Frank's death. And Frank's death wasn't my only *no*. I have shared some of the others with you. I have a unique perspective, because my life is different and unique from anyone else's. As is yours. This is true when I speak as well. There are many other excellent speakers and writers. But what I have to say is mine and mine alone. How I say it, what I say, may reach someone who couldn't be reached by any other person. The same is true with you.

Celebrate your uniqueness. Bless your scars— even your weaknesses. Whatever your scar, whatever your uniqueness, find a point of thankfulness. Out of the turmoil and despair of feeling less than adequate, you can create a place of beauty—a solemn place of quietude—where you can retreat for strength and comfort.

When the scars of life surface, some anticipated, most not, it's important to keep in mind that you have a lot of company—millions of others have and are experiencing your type of pain and/or disappointment. I know that this doesn't seem possible when you feel so down, so out and sometimes as if life is just not worth living.

Many "step" programs have been created to move individuals and groups along with life's situations— whether it's alcohol or drug abuse, excess weight, lost children, death of loved ones, work terminations, divorce—the list expands and extends in all directions. Most cross over and include common steps/commandments to get your life back on track, to begin building your foundation of living once again.

In the many books that I have written, I find myself writing and speaking around a series of points to live by, to heal by, to thrive by. This one is no exception. Often I present these points in a Decalogue format—"The Ten Commandments of . . ." It's easier to remember and my audiences, whether they are readers or listeners, respond to their simplicity. With that in mind, I pass my commandments for overcoming adversity on to you:

THE TEN COMMANDMENTS FOR
OVERCOMING ADVERSITY

### Be True to Yourself

In my book, *The Confidence Factor* (MasterMedia, 1990), "Being True to Yourself" became The First Commandment in building confidence. It holds true in just about any situation. When you stray from the "little voice" from within, it is amazing how out of sync you can and will get. Being true to yourself allows you to open up, be honest, defer suggestions, recommendations, even relationships that "don't fit" with who you are and what you are about.

When you are surrounded by pain and disappointment, it is so easy, in fact, often the norm, to be pulled in multiple directions. Advice may come from every corner, usually spoken in a louder voice than the one you carry internally. You may even feel that you don't know who you are, that your life and everything surrounding it are off balance. Slow down. Take time to be with yourself. Work on your self-talk, your self-worth, meditate and pray. Give your inner voice the opportunity, and permission, to guide and nurture you. It's there. And with it, is God.

### Have a Sense of Humor

When the clouds are the darkest, even considering laughing at anything may seem totally inappropriate. But is it? My sense of humor has helped me in the bleakest of times.

Laughter is one of the best medicines available—and it's free! So much has been written on the need for laughter in our lives, especially in times of illness and pain. When Frank died, my sister-in-law, Linda Vessey, flew in from Colorado with her daughter Shelby a few days before the memorial service.

What a godsend Shelby was. Not yet three, she didn't carry sadness with her, at least, not for long. Rather, she laughed, played with the animals, sang songs—Shelby was a ray of sunshine in our hurricane of pain. Her childlike joy of everyday life played a critical part in the beginning steps of our healing.

When Frank's eulogy was given by his favorite teacher and counselor, Karen Friedman, everyone in the church laughed—and cried. We were reminded of some of the crazy things he had done and how he had brought laughter and joy to so many. Sheryl and I both looked at each other and said at the same time, "There is something wrong, we shouldn't be feeling good at a time like this!"

The humor that was interjected in September of 1983 can still be remembered today by many who attended the service. It was a key ingredient in lifting the dark clouds surrounding all of us. It was a tremendous source of good medicine to and for me.

And it's a surprise ingredient for many at the most unexpected times. The Reverend Dr. John Snyder reminded his congregation that funeral parlors are not the places one goes for decorating tips. He also had the "opportunity" to preside over one of the most memorable funerals—that of a man who had weighed many, many hundreds of pounds.

A tractor had to be used to move the specially constructed coffin to the gravesite. So far, so good. That was, until a crucial balance problem surfaced. And then the unspeakable happened. When the family arrived, the coffin started to slip. In the best Laurel and Hardy fashion, it slid—not into the gravesite, but down, down the hill. At first they were aghast—and then, a few smiles surfaced, followed by snickers and finally by outright belly laughs. You can bet that no one will ever forget that service!

## Take Care of Yourself

This is tough—especially when you feel so rotten. The last thing you may want to do is think about eating, sleeping, exercising—even stretching your mind. When times are rough, it's necessary to stop, take a deep breath and tell yourself that you value *you*. And that you are needed, wanted and cared for. When you hurt, it's normal to feel the opposite.

One of the surest ways to take care of yourself is to surround yourself and your family with *positive reinforcement*. People who are negative, whether they are family, "friends" or outsiders, are not needed. Negative energy begets more negative energy. It permeates the air, your entire environment, even your very being. Look closely at who you are with—do they create positive or negative energy? If you aren't sure, the answer is probably the latter—not a good sign.

If you feel that you are a failure, nine times out of ten, the odds are that you will create a self-fulfilling prophecy. But, if you think you're a winner, when you do fail, you are able to pick up the broken pieces, learn from them—and keep right on moving. The Bible encourages us to "Think about things that are pure and lovely, and dwell on the fine, good things in others. Think about all you can praise God for and be glad about them" (Philippians 4:8).

Negativeness drains whatever thoughts and energy you have going for you at the present time. Moving on means moving on, not being held back. The energy suckers of life destroy just about everything in their path. You need energy boosters, particularly now when you are more vulnerable, not people and more experiences that will be and are a drain on you.

## Expand Your Relationship with Others

Indeed, no man or woman is an island. We need each other—I need you as much as you need me. And most importantly, all of us need to value the ones closest to us instead of taking them for granted—again, the norm for many.

When adversity surfaces, it is quite common to withdraw, to become a quasi-hermit, to put on a mask —sometimes to put up a front that "all is well." It's not—why pretend it is? Now more than ever is the time to reach out—ask for help, for support, for love, for caring, for understanding, yes, even for prayers.

This does not mean that you become a walking doomsayer, that you release negatives from every pore of your body and mind. If you did, you would become the energy drainer/sucker of and for everyone with whom you come in contact. A "persona-non-grata" is someone from whom others will want to turn away.

Rather, it means that you are open with your pains and hurt with those who know you as a person, who also know your accolades and bravos of life—those who can help bring a balance to where you are in the present.

Expanding your relationships with others during times when pains and disappointments surround you gives those who care for you the opportunity to provide what you need the most—a support system from people who love, care, support and are non-judgmental—your true friends.

### Give and Receive Love

There's an old and very familiar saying, "Love isn't love until you give it away." Sayings become adages because they are true. Remember how it felt when you received an unexpected note, call or a gift from someone? Sometimes it is a close friend, at others, just an acquaintance, even someone you may not know! It can make your day!

With the speaking and writing that I do, I often get letters, letters that tell me I have made a difference in someone's life—either by sharing one of my hurts, my pains, my joys, my fears, my successes, even my failures. Someone has connected with some part of me. I save all these letters in a file—my "nice letter" file. They are a constant reminder of what life is about— giving and receiving love.

Each year, Frank gave me a special gift. He would do a *super/duper,* as he called it, cleaning of his room— usually an area of our home that could be classified as a major disaster. And he always did it on the same day— Mother's Day. Each year we made quite a big deal of it! When my memories of missing Frank circulate within me, it's not his birthday nor the day he died that sur- faces—it's the memory of this incredible amount of en- ergy expended for me. Sometimes it was little boy pride that he would display. At other times he was quite boastful. This was his gift of love to me. The memories still make me laugh.

## Stretch Your Mind

I believe that one of God's challenges to each of us is to change—to continue to stretch ourselves, to try to learn something new. It's like rejuvenating your brain cells, even giving them a new lease on life. Otherwise, you get stuck. Stuck in old ways, old habits, old thoughts. As the years pass, your stuckness is like being surrounded with cement—it takes a gigantic jackhammer to break you loose. That gigantic jackhammer may come in the form of a catastrophic event.

Learning something new creates fantastic free- doms—opening doors and windows to areas, concepts and ideas that you may not have ventured into before. It allows you to transform some of your old wishes—"I wish I could play the piano; I wish I knew how to speak another language; I wish I knew how to paint; I wish I knew more about other cultures, I wish I knew how to communicate better with my kids; I wish . . . I wish . . . I wish"—into real goals.

You can learn to play the piano, to speak another language, to paint, about foreign lands, to communicate better—if you really want to. A wish is longing for something and never getting it. A goal is achieving what you set out to get, with a plan to get there. By stretching yourself and transforming wishes into goals, you will find yourself propelled forward. This is an exciting—and sometimes scary—possibility. As you move forward, you will be amazed at the changes and your outlook on the purpose in life.

### Reach Out . . . and Touch Someone

Everyone needs contact with another. And that includes you. It is well documented that without touch and holding, babies do not thrive. Adults are no different. We need to be told that we are cared for, both verbally and physically. Hugs can do wonders. So does a phone call or a note that says, "I'm thinking about you"; "I miss you" or "I love you."

It seems that as we grow older, we are more inhibited in expressing our feelings. Think of a small child— a child who very quickly lets you know if whatever you are doing or proposing to do is liked, or disliked, wanted or desired.

My two-and-one-half-year-old grandson Frankie has no qualms about letting me know what he thinks or wants. He also is very bold in his request for a "kiss" if he feels he has a hurt on his body. He asks, and he gets. What an enormous power I have when all I have to do is give him a hug and a kiss and his world is so much better—at least to him. And to me. Somewhere along the line of growing up, we withdraw and hesitate to let others know what our needs are—a kiss and hug here, a kind word there.

Reaching out is a two-way street—it's both receiving and giving. The more you learn to give—of yourself, your time, your talents, your energy—the more you can and will receive from others. It's like love and marriage, pain and adversity, even peanut butter and jelly—if you give, you will get. They go together.

## Come Out and Play

If there ever was a time to play, being in the middle of adversity is one of them. Yet, for some, it is almost sacrilegious to let play, humor and laughter cross one's mind, much less activate any of us. Remember that humor is one of the best medicines around. It has the remarkable ability to bring diverse groups together with laughter. Laughter and music have been medically proven to create changes in your body that can combat illness and depression.

There was always a lot of play in our house as the kids grew up. It hasn't changed any, especially with frequent visits with our young grandson. In fact, John and I are having a great time playing with Frankie— we know he loves the interaction. We feel we love it even more.

Twenty-three years separated the births of the two Franks—Frank the son and Frankie the grandson.

There are four years stretched from Frank's death to his nephew's birth. And yet, I see a lot in common with these two boys—both play with their toys quite similarly; both are attracted to cars—any car. Both make up silly names for things, are caring and giving, laugh frequently, love to be read to and play hard. The Franks in my life have continued to remind me to stop and smell the roses, to laugh and play along the way.

### Develop Your Relationship with God

Without developing a relationship with God, the other commandments won't be maximized. On a long-term basis, nothing will give you the peace and joy and love that a relationship and dialogue with God will provide. He alone can satisfy the spiritual hunger that gnaws at your heart.

Take some time each day, if you are not doing so already, to be with yourself. And with God. I try to take time the first thing in the morning. I read the Bible and something inspirational. Then I talk *with* God and *to* God, sharing my heartaches, my fears, my joys, my experiences. I have found Him to be a great companion—someone whom I don't, indeed cannot, hide from! By both beginning and ending my day with Him, I find it a superb way to ground myself—it certainly beats the negative news of the world and puts me in a fabulous mindset for whatever the day unfolds or for whatever it has already revealed.

Granted, there are some days that I would like to put in rewind and then eject, not allowing them to enter my real world. Unfortunately, I don't have the option—and neither do you. I have, though, learned to trust in my relationship with God, and to have faith that I will be able to handle what gets served on my plate.

## Walk with Faith

All of us are aware of the horrendous damage and mayhem hurricanes, earthquakes, floods and tornadoes cause—death, families and friends splitting up, destruction of property costing billions of dollars. Pain and suffering abounds. Yet, each city rebuilds, families and friends bind together, the economy rises once again. Why? Because a foundation exists, a foundation that may be battered, but is there, nonetheless.

Each of us has that foundation; it may be covered with the crumbled debris of our past; it may be layered with the debris of the present; but there is some rock to begin to rebuild on. The foundation of faith is as great a rock as you will find to rebuild and restructure your life. It's not a foundation that you will visually see as you do a house's foundation. Rather, your faith foundation builds with your inner daily time with God, with your prayers. Faith, to me, is like the wind—I can't see it, but I can feel it. And, I can see its effects.

Faith becomes the working power in your prayers, part of your strength. With it, nothing is impossible. Without it, you remain in the dark. Lost.

A few years ago, the football teams from the universities of Syracuse and Alabama were down to the final minutes with Syracuse leading by three points. The ball was in Alabama's possession and the team was within scoring distance. On the fourth down, the coach opted to go for the field goal versus an attempt for a touchdown—the difference between winning and tying the score.

The fans viewed it as taking the easy way out and sent over 2,000 neckties to the coach for what they perceived as "choking up" under the pressure. This man's name was mud on campus. Not missing a beat, the coach signed each and turned around and sold them for $100 a piece to the alumni, donating the much needed $20,000 received to the football team! Overcoming adversity, whatever the adversity is, is achieved in a variety of shapes and forms.

You may be thinking that these commandments seem like common sense. You are right—they are. The problem is, though, common sense is not so common. When you are in the depths of pain, adversity and disappointment, it's difficult to let any sense through, much less the common variety!

If you build on the foundation of these commandments, you'll be strong enough to weather any storm that comes your way.

# 6

# Finding and
# Keeping Faith

Several years ago, I was critically ill, a victim of an infection which turned out to be what is known today as classic symptoms from the Dalkon Shield. Thousands of women shared my illness—some died, some had just minor problems.

I was of the first group—so sick. My doctors did not know what was wrong; my insides seemed to be fusing together as the infection raged throughout my body. Parts of me ruptured internally before anyone really realized that I was in crisis. I was dying. I could feel my body weakening and my mind slipping.

The doctors didn't know what to make of the mess they found on the operating table. This was the third set of doctors, the other two pooh-poohing my claims of belly pain, of prolonged menstrual bleeding. They made me feel so stupid, like such a little girl, like a hypochrondriac.

Because no one gave me permission to be sick, I kept returning to work. A friend called to ask how I was feeling. I told her my saga of the previous two doctors and she insisted that I see hers, a doctor who had completed a successful cancer surgery on her the year before.

I told her that the previous two doctors said that my complaints were minor, that I was imagining the bladder infection I suspected. They even told me that my problems stemmed from constipation, but I knew different. My friend said that she didn't like the sound of my voice, that there wasn't strength in it. She begged me to see her doctor, a man she had been referred to by a colleague of her dentist husband. He was a pathologist and this particular surgeon only did surgery when it was absolutely necessary. It was the kind of referral you and I normally don't receive.

I followed my friend's advice and made the appointment. A few days later I cancelled it. The second doctor had called me and said that he thought I might have kidney stones—something that I had heard was indeed painful. As one of the world's greatest rationalizers, I jumped at the suggestion—kidney stones it must be. Tests were scheduled for the following week. Meanwhile, the third doctor's nurse called me back, "Why did you cancel your appointment for later this morning?" I told her. She reminded me of the ongoing bleeding and the pain.

The night before, I had been racked with pain. That morning I actually did feel better, at least in comparison as I spoke with her. She insisted that I come in. I was dumbfounded. Someone cared, actually cared!

For whatever reason, I decided to reinstate the appointment and asked my husband to drive me. As I met the new doctor in his office, giving him my medical history, I started to slide from my chair, laying my head on his desk. I knew I was in trouble, real trouble, and so did he.

I was rushed to the examining room and to this day, only vaguely remember parts of what happened. I remember the doctor taking my hand and saying to me, "Don't you feel these lumps in your stomach?" I remember his extreme seriousness, his directions to his nurse, who was his wife, to help me dress and bring me back to his office. I remember seeing John there when I entered and the doctor saying, "I normally do not like to meet someone for the first time and immediately say you need a hysterectomy right away. I want you to go straight to the hospital. You don't belong on your feet. We are calling to schedule surgery for tomorrow."

Surgery—a hysterectomy?! I was only thirty years old. John and I were planning on having a child together this year. How could this be happening to me? To us? He said I had a huge fibroid tumor. It was a six-month pregnancy size. I knew my tummy had been pooching out a little, but this? Now? Impossible!

Sylvia, the nurse, came back and said that the hospital couldn't schedule nonemergency surgery for the next day, Saturday. "Could I go home," I asked, "and be with my kids over the weekend?" Still thinking we were dealing with a tumor, the doctor said, "Yes, as long as you stay in bed and check into the hospital Sunday."

I was relieved. Something was wrong with me; it wasn't in my head, a figment of my active imagination. I had permission to be sick . . . finally. John took me back to my office and I told my manager I would be out for a few weeks. Feigning that I was semi-OK, I cooked dinner that night. I explained to the kids that I would be gone for a few days and described the surgery I was to have. I told them I needed to rest over the weekend until John took me back to the hospital on Sunday.

When I lay down that Friday night I barely moved until Sunday, until it was time to go to the hospital. I knew something was wrong, awfully wrong, but I didn't know exactly what. The second doctor called and was angry at me for going to another and agreeing to hospitalization and surgery. To appease him, I promised to get another opinion, which I never did. My inner sense told me that I was finally in the right physician's hands. I felt that Everett Eaton, M.D. was God's gift to the *no* I was surrounded by with other doctors.

We lived at the top of a windy road in the hills. More than a hundred homes were set back in our little community, with the annual pot luck meeting scheduled that Sunday at our home. I told John to let it continue, that there were plenty of workers and I would stay in bed.

By Sunday I was floating in and out, barely aware of my surroundings, and hardly able to walk. I said my goodbyes to the kids, hugging them and extracting promises of good behavior while I was gone. By the time I was admitted to the hospital I felt I was going to explode. A wheelchair became my only means of transportation.

The "routine" hysterectomy was anything but routine. The doctors were stunned when they made the initial incision. They had never seen anything like what they saw presented. They were sure I had cancer of the bladder. My colon had ruptured and my insides were like layered wet tissues, almost impossible to pull apart—to unstick.

The hysterectomy that was scheduled didn't occur—it took the growing team of doctors three hours just to separate my fused organs. The prognosis wasn't good. More like, "Let's close her up and get out of here."

Several weeks later, I went home—tubes out of every part of me, no feeling below my waist. I had to learn to walk again, to eat, to take care of myself. And my family—I was the primary breadwinner—was in shock. How could I be so sick, so helpless? How were we going to eat? Pay the mortgage?

There were days when I felt I got nowhere. Then there were others when giant leaps occurred. When I woke up in the morning, it was a joy to look out my bedroom window and see the oaks that surrounded our house. It was as if nature was trying different combinations of her paintbrush. It was a pleasure to open my eyes and feel the rays dance around me.

Months later, my feelings returned, my body was healing, really healing. To this day, I know that there were tasks I had to complete, that God wasn't done with me. He had plans that the ensuing years would reveal layer by layer.

While I was in the hospital, another classic experience took place. When I am asked to describe that experience today, fifteen years later, it is as clear as if it happened an hour ago. One moment, I was lying in my bed talking to the doctor, the next, I literally slipped from my physical body, just like the Casper the Friendly Ghost cartoons I watched as a child on TV. It seemed I was floating above the scene at the top of the room. In those few moments, I moved from intense pain to a serene state. I was warm in faith, all pain gone and surrounded by light. I definitely preferred where I was as I observed the doctors in their attempt to revive me. It was a wonderful sensation!

And then, as quickly as I drifted out of my body, I was back, as if there was a reason to be here, not to have died. Within a few weeks, I felt I knew the answer. In fact, there were two answers. The first was a closure—closure with my children's father, a man who had been an abusive husband and a mediocre father. The phone call I had with him evolved around his parenting or lack of it, his relationships with adults, or lack of them.

My hope for him was that he would get some badly needed therapy, that he would stay away from booze. If he didn't, his present marriage would falter and his other children would become estranged, as ours had been from him.

The second "purpose" for not completing my death journey was my children. I hadn't really made plans for their total care, just assuming that nothing would ever happen to me, as so many parents do routinely. Probably as you do—and have. I called my "heart-Mom" Joyce and asked her if she would be there for my kids if something happened to me. To be there emotionally and financially, to guide them spiritually, to protect them from the wild card—their father, her son. Legally, their father could regain custody of them. "Of course," she said. Shelley, Frank and Sheryl were her first grandchildren—she had a special place for them in her heart. I have the same special feeling for my first grandchild, Frankie.

Both calls were made while I was still in the hospital. I felt a sense of urgency in making them, and a sense of completion afterward. I still didn't know why I was so ill; neither did John, nor the doctor. We all knew, though, that I had been in a life-threatening situation . . . I learned later that the doctors didn't expect me to live, and that the culprit was the Dalkon Shield.

My near-death/out-of-body experience parallels what others have shared after their experiences. I do know that when death occurs, the pain is gone and with it light, illuminating light, envelopes you—it did me. And it has enveloped others.

One of my favorite songs is "In This Very Room" by Ron and Carol Harris. Every time I hear it, the melody lingers for days, sometimes weeks. "In this very room, there is quite enough love for all of us."

I was entranced when I first heard it sung by four of my friends—so simple, so beautiful and yet so profound.

As I sat in church one Sunday, the sermon seemed based on this song. Looking around the sanctuary, I was taken by all the things that had occurred to me in this very room.

After years of nonchurch attendance, I had reconnected with the community church when the need for a service after Frank's death occurred. In this very room, hundreds came—our friends, Frank's friends, his sister's friends, relatives, even the curious. All were hurting, all were seeking reasons, all were offering support for each other.

In this very room, we honored John's father who died just a few months after Frank did. It was hard for Shelley and Sheryl to return once again to focus on the dead. Yet, somehow, they did. We all did.

In this very room my husband became a Christian after Frank's death, after claiming for all the years I had known him that he was agnostic. When John finally welcomed God into his heart, he became a new man, and our marriage, a new marriage. When Frank died, we were in trouble, separating for a period, living in the same house yet not living there. In this very room, I remarried my husband—a much better, stronger and caring marriage than our first one.

In this very room, daughter Sheryl married. And in this very room, my grandson was baptized while I stood in front of the congregation as the representative elder with our pastor.

Yes, "In This Very Room" is an important melody for me, for this room has carried great pain, fear, hope, joy, love and faith. And faith brings it all together. All the pieces fall into place as in a master puzzle, a master plan.

As I write this I can't help but be reminded of one of the lessons demonstrated in my favorite room by our pastor, Mark Goodman Morris. The message was simple, yet deep. God is calling us to live on the edge. I have heard others say these words; you probably have too. But this last time I heard them they stuck. When we get "stuck" in life's problems, when we think we can't get out, it's time to live on the edge—the edge of faith.

At the burning bush, Moses was in just such a spot. He was stuck. Really stuck. While he was still in Egypt, he saw the injustice and oppression that his people lived under. You may recall the story—he saw an Egyptian knock one of his Hebrew brothers to the ground. He was furious! Taking justice into his own hands, he killed the Egyptian. He thought his people would understand, but they didn't. Right then and there, afraid of being executed, Moses fled to the backside of the desert. He was ostracized, alone. And he was probably confused as to why God had allowed this to happen. After all, he had been living in the Pharaoh's own house as one of his sons. He was a man of high position. Yet he was reduced to running from his own household as a criminal because he stood up for what he thought was right and just.

Moses ended up out in the middle of nowhere, tending sheep instead of leading his people. He was stuck. And not only was he stuck, he was also afraid. Somewhere between killing the Egyptian and running to exile, Moses lost his courage—but not his call. *He* may have forgotten his determination to free his fellow Hebrews from slavery, but God hadn't. God appeared to Moses in the middle of a burning bush—it was time to get Moses unstuck. It was time to get Moses to stand on the edge of faith—and move forward. "Who me?" asks Moses. "Yes, you," replies God. No more hiding, no more sitting around tending sheep. There were bigger sheep to be shepherded. And it was time to shepherd them out of Egypt.

God didn't ask Moses to do this through "blind faith." God gave Moses proof, through a series of miracles, that He would be at Moses' side, helping him, guiding him. God made Himself known in a tangible way to Moses, so when things got tough back in Egypt, Moses was prepared, by faith in God, to withstand the trials. When Moses was stuck, God called him to "live on the edge" and have faith to forge ahead. Quite a lesson, indeed!

In this very room that day, I was reminded that God is there when we get stuck. He helps us whether we're on the edge, the ledge, in the wedge, even a hedge—I know, I've been in all those places!

## Faith Is Tangible

Often, you see faith described by the metaphor of people walking into the unknown—stepping into a deep, dark fog—and "believing," without seeing, that something will be there to hold them up. You may have participated in a "faith fall" or a "faith walk" where you were blindfolded and guided around by someone else—not knowing where you were or where you were going. In a blind fall, you are encouraged to fall backward, and forward, and someone, you have no idea who, will catch you. I don't think that this concept is totally accurate. Or true. Contrary to popular belief, faith is tangible. Real. Touchable. The faith described in the Bible isn't blind—as seen by the story of Moses and exemplified in the story of Abraham.

Abraham is known as "the father of faith." He sets a good example of tangible faith. The faith He had in God was faith in a God who proved Himself. How? In Genesis, God visits Abraham. In the context of that visit, God makes a "blood covenant" with him.

Now, Abraham knew something about this blood covenant that isn't readily obvious when you read the Bible. He knew that a blood covenant was *unbreakable*. In Abraham's time, two men made a blood covenant by going through an elaborate ritual to pledge their lives to one another. This series of rituals bound these two men together in an agreement of "faith." American Indians used to do something similar when they cut their wrists and mingled their blood together. I can even remember pricking my finger as a kid with a friend— we would rub our bloody fingers together—blood sisters to the end!

Through this unbreakable pledge, two men would vow to help one another, take on each other's debts, fight each other's battles, feed each other's families if one were killed unexpectedly in battle—in short, they covenanted their lives whole-heartedly and unselfishly to one another. This is what God did with Abraham.

While Abraham slept, God made a covenant with him, going through familiar rituals, to pledge to Abraham that He would take care of him and his family. In the context of that promise, God told Abraham that he would have descendants as plentiful as the sand and stars. All Abraham did was take up God's good offer.

Abraham wasn't believing in some dark abyss of faith. He knew that if God was making a blood covenant with him that it was unbreakable. It was irrefutable proof that God was worthy of his faith. God could be trusted.

Others, like Rahab the harlot, are heroes of faith found in the Bible. Rahab—a prostitute—is singled out and praised for her faith. She was living in the city of Jericho. Joshua sent two spies to check out the city before they were to conquer it. They found their way to Rahab's house. When some men of Jericho came looking for them, she hid them, protecting them from discovery and harm. Why? Because she had heard of the great deeds of the God of the Israelites. She tells the spies what she's heard: how God had dried up the waters of the Red Sea so the Israelites could pass through on dry land; how they had utterly destroyed their enemies. She heard about it. And she believed it. To her, God's protection and help for the people of Israel was tangible, visible proof that God was real. God calls it faith.

The tangible proof we have today is just as irrefutable. Just as real. Just as tangible. My faith is not based on some blind leap into darkness. It is based on a calculated step into the light—the light that God promises, unequivocally. By opening my heart to God, I have entered into a covenant with Him—a new covenant. This covenant tells me that He will turn my sorrows into joy. It tells me that in my darkest nights I will be able to find Him. And I will be able to grow, heal and turn to reach back to others to pull them to the light.

## Faith through Trials

Faith doesn't always mean you see the promise, the *yes*, right away. Abraham had to wait twenty years. But it does mean standing on something tangible, the tangible promises of a God who is there, and believing Him in the face of uncertain circumstances, and sometimes in the face of out-and-out evil.

Hindsight is always fantastic—it is amazing how right on we can be when time has elapsed. The wisdom of experience comes when we look back. And the perspective of hindsight allows us to weigh the pros and cons, the good and the bad, the ugly and the beautiful—all things that at first glance, at first experience, may be cloaked. They may, in fact, be the opposite of what we initially felt or saw. Haven't we all been fooled at least once—or more?

There are those alive today who have stood patiently in trying circumstances—in faith. In pre-*Perestroika* Russia, the faith of Christians and Jews carried them through extreme hardship and persecution. Stories of their courage and bravery as they endured physical torture, psychological pressures, deprivation and hardship have been told and retold. Yet they stood. Unmoved. In faith. Believing.

The Zernovs were just such a family. They were Soviet Christians who put their faith in a tangible God, regardless of their circumstances.

Jenny Zernov Gordeuk, one of eight Zernov children, recalls going to school one day in Leninist Russia during the 1920s. She never expected what followed. The teacher asked her if she believed in God. Jenny recalls her ten-year-old self as being stunned. "Why yes," she replied, "we believe in God." What surprised

Jenny further was to hear her teacher quote scripture. Then the teacher asked her, "Do you believe that God is a Spirit and those who worship him must worship him in spirit and in truth?" Again she responded, "Yes." The teacher turned to the class. She began to mock Jenny, telling the other students how stupid it was to believe in God, any God for that matter. "We know, and science proves," continued the teacher, "that there is no God." Ten-year-old Jenny remained steadfast in her faith, encouraged by the deep faith of her mother, of her family.

Eventually, through extreme taxation, the Zernovs were stripped of most of their possessions. All that remained were the barest necessities of life. Just living on a daily basis became an immense struggle. The younger children weren't allowed to attend school—forced out by the government; the older ones, who were preparing to become teachers, would have to teach that there was no God. In the Zernov family this was not an option. Their faith was strong.

Still, Jenny recalls her family's life of extreme hardship did not get them down. They remained joyful and continued to thank God for what they had, rather than complain about what they didn't have. Through their trials, her mother quoted the scripture, "Seek ye first the kingdom of God . . . and all these things will be added unto you." In the Zernov family, that was how they lived.

Unbelievably, after much perseverance, much hardship and no answers, God gave them a *yes* behind their *no*. Years later, relatives from Wisconsin sent them tickets to come to the United States. Because of their financial poverty, because the children were no longer in school, because they were no longer a "promising family," the Soviet officials were glad to see them leave. Having been stripped of their material possessions— something that on the surface may have seemed over- whelmingly bad and was most certainly difficult—was the very stripping process that "bought" them their freedom. Poverty had made them rich! The very thing that brought this family pain, also brought them joy. Their *yes* became their ticket to America.

## Faith Reaches Out

Through their release, many others have been set free. The Zernovs' tangible faith has reached out dra- matically to transform the lives of others. Through their own spiritual beliefs that are alive today with each successful generation, and also through Jenny's continued efforts to help other Soviet Christians escape persecution, they are bringing others to a new life of religious freedom in the United States. They found faith. They kept their faith through disappointment and harassment. And that faith was multiplied. Their faith was not just something tangibly perceived—it was also tangibly doled out to others. True faith, if it is really faith, reaches out. Touching. Caring. Supporting.

Mother Teresa and godliness are synonymous. She is one of the most visibly godly women living today. Her work in India is known throughout the world. Her compassionate care for the lowest class citizens of that land has been widely recognized. She has been hon- ored with a Nobel Peace Prize. What kind of faith has caused her to give up all earthly comforts and plea- sures to sacrifice her life totally for others?

In a television interview on *The 700 Club* with Scott Hatch she was asked what it is that she prays for herself. Her reply was astounding. She doesn't. She doesn't pray for herself. She only prays for others and allows Jesus and others to pray for her. Mother Teresa trusts totally in God's absolute love for her. She says Jesus will pray for her—and she rests in that knowledge. She believes God. There's no striving, no competition for His attention. She knows she has it, by faith. Her faith sets her free from self-preoccupation to reach out to "the lowliest of the low"—to God Himself as expressed through others. She has found faith. And the entire world has witnessed faith through her.

Jesus is reported to have said, "You are the world's light—a city on a hill, glowing in the night for all to see. Don't hide your light! Let it shine for all; let your good deeds glow for all to see, so that they will praise your heavenly Father." This describes Mother Teresa. All who know her recognize her good deeds, her compassionate contribution to humanity. An entire world looks at her, and whether they believe in God or not, they say to themselves, "This is what it means to be a Christian." And they respect her for it. Her faith, as evidenced by her good works, brings praise to God.

Several years ago James Taylor sang a song that states this message very simply, yet poignantly: "shower the people you love with love, show them the way that you feel . . ." Faith is expressed through loving those around you. Showing them God's love. Comforting them, caring for them, giving of yourself to them, challenging them and just plain being there.

The Bible tells us that when everything as we know it is gone, three things will remain: faith, hope and love. The three are intimately linked. They are facets of the diamond of one's life in God. Faith gives us hope, hope gives us love, love gives us faith. Amazingly, the Bible says that when we run into problems and trials we should be happy about it—we should rejoice! Imagine that. Yet we're told that trials are good for us because they teach us to be patient. And patience is what develops strength of character in us. We're also told that trials help us trust God more each time we, in hindsight, see the end results. "Then, when that happens, we are able to hold our heads high no matter what happens and know that all is well, for we know how dearly God loves us, and we feel this warm love everywhere within us because God has given us the Holy Spirit to fill our hearts with his love" (Romans 5:5).

The standard of faith that needs to be raised is not a standard of prosperity and wealth. It's not a standard of condemnation or rebuke. Rather, it is a standard of integrity and compassion. These are the standards of faith. Faith is the standard against evil, injustice and oppression in the world. For it is in loving and reaching out to others, it is in finding and keeping faith, that we can change our world. This is not to suggest that faith is a compensation for loss or pain or tragedy. But it is an outgrowth, a tangible outgrowth. It is what makes life worth living.

### "Surprise Me . . ."

Faith is also rewarded with surprises. Just as it is impossible to please God without faith, it is also impossible to have faith without being happily and joyously surprised by God.

Sarah learned this when God told her husband Abraham that she would have a baby. This baby would arrive when others their age would be in the great-great-grandparent role. While the Bible says that Abraham believed God, it tells us that Sarah laughed. She thought it was hysterical. "What? Have a baby at my age? You've got to be kidding!"

Even though she laughed, the writer to the Hebrews states that Sarah was a person of great faith—she believed that God would do what He said He would do. Her faith was met with a joyful surprise from God. It was a surprise only He could give her, since she was too old to have a baby without a miracle from God. To many women, having a baby past the "normal" child-bearing years, comes as quite a shock. Sarah and Abraham were shocked. And surprised.

When Suzie, a bright, talented, vivacious woman, was in her mid-twenties, she wanted earnestly to be married. She felt she had much to offer a man and to bring to a marriage. She had taught second grade and she had begun a new career in children's television after earning her master's degree in communication. Even so, Suzie suffered through three very disappointing engagements. Each time, her fiance would tell her that it was "God's will" that they marry—each time, God apparently changed His mind. Somehow this never made sense to her.

Up until this point, Suzie had always been so sure that she had known God's plan for her life. Up until now, she had lived a "charmed" life—everything had been picture perfect. Now, something had mixed up the plan, something that was out of her control—and she didn't know how to get back on track.

Suzie was understandably discouraged over this repetitive pattern of broken engagements—yet surprisingly hopeful. She knew God loved her enough to give her a husband. There was no question about that.

Yet she couldn't understand why this rejection kept happening to her or what she was doing wrong.

Coming home after graduation, after her third broken engagement, Suzie was numb. Sad. But also expectant. She was coming home. This was a starting over. A new beginning.

One day in a church class on Christian dating, Suzie was sitting with her back to a handsome young man, softly crying as the leader spoke. She thought to herself, *This guy must think I'm a real wimp.* After class and right before the service began, a friend introduced her to him—J.T. She thought to herself, *Yeah, he'll probably ask me out, fall madly in love with me, tell me it's God's will that we marry, and then leave—just like all the others.*

As she was sitting next to J.T., the pastor instructed everyone to join hands in prayer. While holding his hand, Suzie decided to stop letting her imagination run wild. She didn't want to think ahead. She determined to take every thought captive and not even try to guess what was next. Suzie looked up at God and prayed, "Surprise me! Just surprise me!" And you know what? He did! Her faith and patience were rewarded. Today Suzie is happily married to J.T. and she has two darling boys who continue to keep her surprised! Her life, she feels, is a direct result of her growing faith.

## When All Else Goes Wrong

Like Suzie, there are times when each of us questions our worth—our own and that of those around us. There are times when life doesn't seem worth living, there appears nowhere to turn, or no one to turn to, to lean on, to trust. Yet there is.

Several years ago, I received a call from one of my agents. He told me he was representing a woman I may have read about in the paper. He shared that she had had a rough time, that she was due to be in California in a few months to serve a six-month term in prison on perjury charges. He believed that she was innocent, that she had been set up. He asked me if I would call her. I did.

Since that first phone call, a whole new world has opened to me. We all read about politics in the news, hearing and watching on radio and TV, but few of us really get to hear "the rest of the story" as broadcaster Paul Harvey so eloquently states.

That phone call led to my placing another phone call and beginning a friendship that didn't bring the two of us together physically until my first visit to the women's prison in Vacaville, California. My new friend was Rita Lavelle, who had held a highly visible position in the United States Environmental Protection Agency—the EPA. She was one of six assistant administrators while Anne Burford was head of the EPA during a portion of Ronald Reagan's term as President. Rita had been found guilty on four counts of perjury. She was accused by four different congressional committees of lying about a meeting date.

During Rita's hearings, no one could find the missing memos that verified that meetings had or had not occurred. Her prosecutors, assisted through the Department of Justice, had, according to Rita, ". . . orchestrated a twenty-day discrepancy into a major crime." The Department of Justice succeeded in withholding documents for eighteen months that would have verified Rita Lavelle's position. The chief prosecutor claimed that meant she would step into a "big bucks job" in return for lying for industry.

Tragically, none of the so-called "proof" emerged until after Rita spent time in jail. Just moments before the devastating October 1989 earthquake in the Bay Area of Northern California hit, I had just finished a "catch-up chat" with her, checking in just to let her know I care.

I admire her tenacity to keep trying—she really cares about the environment, about toxic waste clean-up, about toxic waste prevention. She shared that she is struggling—struggling to build a business, struggling to be accepted as a legitimate business person, struggling to deal with the injustice of the past.

She shared that there is proof beyond a doubt that she had been framed. Alexia Morrison, a tenacious and bright attorney in Washington D.C., had finally put all the pieces together. She had probed and forced files and materials to be turned over. Today, Rita is still classified as a felon, serving her fifth and final year of probation after the initial jail sentence. The pardon that was promised has not materialized.

Rita's saga has been splashed across the pages of *Time, Newsweek,* just about every paper in the country, and TV shows like *Today.* Most talk about her conviction, but very few are willing even to report new material that supports her. The public, the press, love bad news. Rita's dream is to clear herself. She hopes to some day have the money to support the legal costs to present the new evidence and expose the frame-up. Until then, in the law's eyes, in the public vision, she will remain a felon.

Her ordeal is something that you and I will probably never experience. Throughout it, she has continued to fuel her faith—a faith that has been tested more times than she cares to count. Rita told me that when she was twelve, she had a spiritual vision. It indicated that she would be a major factor in a media event. Unfortunately her vision didn't include all the pain and the ostracism that she has experienced and that hurts so much.

## Believing Without Seeing

"God's Footprints" is a poem about a man, or a woman, who looks back, reflecting over his or her life and discovers that there are two sets of footprints in the sand as life's journey unfolds. One set belongs to the man or the woman, the other to God. In noting a particularly dark period, when everything was going wrong, the person notes that only one set of footprints appears. God is questioned as to why He left during this time of deepest need. God replies, "I never left— for that was the time I carried you through your most trying hour. Those are my footprints." This is life with God. This, too, is faith.

When Jesus and His disciples crossed the lake, a storm buffeted their small boat. All feared, except Jesus, who napped peacefully. When He was awakened, He calmed the storm and then queried His disciples, "Where is your faith?" (Luke 8:25 NIV). His question wasn't meant to chastise. Rather, it was meant to inspire, to encourage His disciples so they would understand that no matter how frightful the storm, no matter how wild the seas, He would always be there to turn to, to trust in, and to help. In the storms of life, we can count on Him.

### Faith Is Positive

When I speak to groups about the critical necessity to create positive energy, usually I ask a member of the audience to come on stage with me for a demonstration. Prior to introducing her to the audience, I tell my "partner" that at the time I direct her, I want her to think one of two thoughts. The first thought is positive—to let anything positive enter her mind. It can be getting a raise, good health, a birth, money, a trip—whatever to her is positive. When I ask her to think this first thought, I want her to feel the thought throughout her body. When she has a "fix" on it, I then ask her to hold out her arm to the side, parallel with the floor. I then instruct her to resist my downward pressure on the extended arm. The result—lots of strength, the arm doesn't go down.

Now it's time for the second thought—total negativism. She is to think anything that makes her feel bad or depressed—poor health, being fired, a divorce, pain—whatever thoughts are negative. I then ask her to hold out the arm the same way, and to resist when I attempt to push it down.

This time there's quite a difference—no resistance. The negative thoughts have depleted her of any energy, of anything positive.

My temporary partner is always surprised, as is the audience, with the results. By evoking the dark side, by seeing just the negative, by not letting the good vibes in, we weaken ourselves.

Although faith is not necessarily positive thinking, faith *is* positive. Faith lends positive strength to our lives in our negative circumstances.

In the Introduction of this book, I told how Frank's death brought me three gifts, with one being that of renewed spirituality. This gift has been one of my most important gifts to be birthed out of his death. In one of the Gospels Jesus says, "I tell you the truth, unless a kernel of wheat falls to the ground and dies, it remains only a single seed. But if it dies, it produces many seeds" (John 12:24 NIV). If the wings of Frank's death could bring forth new life in me and in the lives of those who were deeply touched by his death, then there was a purpose that goes beyond the insanity of this life, beyond the tragedy of the accident. It looks beyond the otherwise senselessness of his departure. This, to me, is finding faith. It's mine to keep.

Finding, keeping and allowing faith to grow is a key ingredient in moving beyond *no,* to allowing the *yes* in. Biblical stories of the past as well as today's modern stories illustrate that when we have felt at our weakest point, help arrived. It's rather like an invading army, marching in and playing a new tune. Not merely does it save or protect us, it re-routes us, directing us in totally new directions—moving us forward to a spiritual vision.

# 7

# God's Touch . . . A Spiritual Vision

One of the ways I used to cope with my emptiness and pain after Frank's death was to go to an exercise class. I could both sweat and cry, figuring no one would notice me.

One night between sessions, one of the instructors came up to me. Tapping me on the shoulder, she said, "I know you don't know who I am, but I know who you are. And I want you to know that my kids will never go out on the bridge again." Initially, I was dumbfounded. What did she mean, "My kids will never go out on the bridge again"? She proceeded to tell me that it was a place where loads of kids hung out—where they partied.

I made some phone calls. The State Police confirmed what she had said—that it was a hang-out. They had attempted to put pressure on Caltrans to close it off—to do something about it before someone got hurt. All they got was no response—no action. Now it was too late. At least for Frank. One side of me never wanted to see that bridge again, nor hear the name, much less see it, to drive on it. The other side, though, told me I had to do something. I could not forgive myself if someone else's child was hurt or killed on the bridge.

Because of what happened, I knew then that I had the power to do something—in fact, I had probably the single most important voice to force action on the old Dumbarton Bridge. My job, my vision, my obsession became to deal with this issue. To force action.

Out of the *no* of Frank's death, I had found faith and kept faith. His death, and this faith, propelled me forward with a spiritual vision—a call—to make this area a safer place for all the other "Franks." It nudged me to help other mothers avoid having to undergo the same anguish and heartbreak that I, my family and Frank's friends had experienced through his tragic death.

That entire year I had carried the memory of Frank with me—close to me. At times I could feel him at my right shoulder, comforting me, encouraging me to forge ahead in the face of a difficult battle with the State to make that bridge area safe.

Caltrans insisted that there had always been a gate to keep trespassers out and that warnings were clearly posted. When we went out to check, there was a gate, but it was tied open. And if untied, it could span only half the entrance. John had climbed mountains in college and was knowledgeable about ropes and knots. He said that the knotted ropes had been there for a long, long time. It was clear that the gate was always tied open.

Two weeks after the accident, Sheryl and I walked out to the end of the bridge—the portion that was rumored to be altered to allow fishing. As we visually surveyed the site, it became clear that this place was frequented by many—soda and beer cans, "picnic" supplies, even baby diapers littered the area.

A lone fisherman was also there. He told us that he often came here after work—his was the swing shift, 3 P.M. to 11 P.M. He verified that it was common to have kids out there goofing off, that rarely were his fishing excursions not infiltrated by the noise of others. He continued that the only time he ever saw anyone official was when a game warden drove out to check his fishing license. Caltrans, the bridge toll personnel and the bridge authorities all knew people—kids— routinely came out to the bridge. It was a mishap waiting to happen. The invitation was already extended! Something had to be done. Now.

I began with phone calls to friends in the press, the radio and TV. One television reporter, Judy Peterson, called me and said that the other side of the bridge was even worse, the side that Caltrans was actively working on. Calls from some of the mothers of Frank's friends came. They, too, had driven out to the site after the accident. They were appalled at the construction/ reconstruction chaos.

Both Judy Peterson and they reported that gates didn't exist and in fact, Judy called to encourage us to go out and take pictures at sunrise, before the crews arrived for work. We did. It was clear that the only existent gates were on the ground—run over daily as trucks and cars drove back and forth doing "their work."

Even so, Caltrans insisted that they always put gates up when no one was there to keep anyone from getting hurt. The lies mounted. There was absolutely no way that they could be put up at night time when the workers went home, much less during the day when others were around.

By then, I felt that the only way to get the State's attention was through its pocketbook. I sued for five million dollars. I knew that if I didn't go after the State, someone else could get hurt. And it had to be with something that would merit their attention, a large amount. We knew that money wouldn't and couldn't replace Frank. We were also skeptical of recovering any—that wasn't the issue. Action was.

The lies compounded—the State kept deluding themselves and trying to keep us away from the site. Three weeks after Frank died, a gate finally went up that actually went across the access to the bridge with a "no trespassing" sign on it. But the gate was setting only in front of the roadway. On either side, a walker or biker had easy access to continue—as though the State decided that a "sidewalk" might be nice. It didn't make sense. If a barrier is going up, then it should be a barrier. Period.

Unfortunately, when tragedy occurs, the "rubber neckers" of life surface. People were curious about the site. Where did it happen? How did it happen? Let's go out there to see why the kids went there! Let's climb too! Needless to say, the State's response wasn't too effective!

Finally, three months after Frank died, the California Assembly voted $4.7 million to demolish the section of the bridge where Frank had fallen. A friend, well connected within Sacramento, California's capitol, called and said that, although "they" would never admit it, it was my pressure via the media and my lawsuit which caused the voting of the funds. One of the TV stations called for an interview after the allocation was announced. They wanted my reaction and also heard that I would be dismissing the lawsuit—who did they hear that from? I had made no announcement about a dismissal.

The following year we watched it blow up—a major closing. A major triumph. Crowds gathered to watch the "event." Our friend and my right hand at work, Jo

Hanley, John and I positioned ourselves directly across from it on a small section of the Bay. Sheryl and Shelley had formed groups with their friends—all of us very private with our thoughts.

It was truly a marvel. Once standing as a monument to engineering, its steel girders all powerful and impenetrable, the great bridge fell swiftly to its grave. A series of detonations exploded its base. It fell down as I imagined Frank had fallen. The entire tower sections merely disappeared into the Bay—once again I saw Frank in my mind's eye, slipping unconsciously into the depths. The experience was quite surreal, as if someone in a penthouse had pushed the elevator button for the lobby. We heard a rumble, delayed a few seconds for time to carry the sound of the dynamite. Then it was gone. The bridge was gone. Just like Frank. Here and real, one instant; enveloped in silence the next. My mission was accomplished. My spiritual vision complete.

About a year after Frank died, I had a vision—a dream in the early morning hours. Frank was in my room, and I sensed Sheryl peripherally. I sat up. Frank asked me why I had waited so long to scatter his ashes. I explained that I had to wait until all the kids came back—that we could only do it once and Kit, his best friend, wasn't coming back from Oklahoma until Christmas time. "Oh," was the response—it wasn't until a few weeks later that I realized Frank was no longer on my right shoulder. His presence was no longer felt. I was angry that he had deserted me. Later I realized why—I no longer needed him to help me get through each day.

To bring the cycle full circle, it was time to get closure on the outstanding lawsuit. My intent was not to get money, but rather to get the State's attention. Mission accomplished. To the surprise of my attorneys, I instructed them to settle the case by covering their costs with the total settlement and then closing it out. Frank had helped me find my faith, he had helped me keep a spiritual vision—and now he could be put to rest. Final rest.

### Are These Lessons?

A former friend wrote to me after Frank's death offering condolences. I called her thanking her for the note. She proceeded to say that I was being "taught a lesson." There was a "lesson" to be learned here—how could she say that? Those words slipped so glibly off of her tongue—yet she had never walked in my shoes. She had never felt my anguish.

The point is, bad times are not dumped on us to teach us a lesson, but lessons do emerge as an aftermath. These lessons become powerful tools in our daily living. God wasn't "teaching me a lesson" by allowing Frank to fall to his death. But He could teach me a lesson *after* Frank's death. I learned to find a *yes* behind God's *no*. I learned how to find a spiritual vision—a purpose—to carry me through the trying months following his accident. And I learned that my voice could count for something—really count. I had a part to play in the destiny of that bridge—a role to carry out in the history of that community. And my role was significant, filled with purpose and meaning.

When so much time is spent wondering why these calamities happen—death, destruction, illness, broken bones, accidents, getting old and infirm—we lose sight of the tremendous potential we have to effect change.

No matter what end of the spectrum our *no* is on, whether it's a big *no* or a little one, as each *no* comes along, it seems like a catastrophe—it's *what is* versus *what I want,* or *what I can't have.* When accidents happen, they aren't an outgrowth of God's wrath, His will or His punishment—most problems, like smog, are man-made. Some are traumatic, some are little bumps. But behind the tragedy of our *no* lies a vision waiting to be birthed.

I'll never forget my next door neighbor's words when Billy died: "It was God's will." Nonsense. I don't accept that. Things just happen. After things happen, though, we must open up and be receptive to the spiritual vision that will come in—if we let it. Not that God made it happen so you could see. But now that it has happened, look, watch, feel, listen for a message to come your way—to find a positive meaning in the event. Something you can learn, that you can grasp, that you can share.

In Frank's case, his death accentuated the fact that we're not indestructible. You can die at nineteen. You are not made of steel; you are not made of rubber, capable of rebounding. You are not invincible. Our "forever" can be one week, three years or nineteen years. You must live each day as if it's all you've got—it could be your last. This lesson hit home for me. I can look back on Frank's death and know I had no unfinished business with Frank. No regrets. We were in harmony with each other. Oh, there were plenty of times when I wanted to wring his neck—kid things that he would pull, mother-son disagreements, parent-child conflicts. Real Life 101.

When Frank left our home that summer night, so full of youthful enthusiasm and hope, there were no left-out sayings or feelings. For the past year all of us had agonized over "career" direction for and with Frank. And then there was his service obligation, something that both John and I felt would be an asset —for discipline and education. Frank had friends in the army and he didn't like what he heard. He really didn't want to go far away, half-way around the world. That ruled out the Marines and Navy. On the day that Frank died, information arrived in the mail from the U.S. Coast Guard. I never opened it, finally throwing it away.

One of the gifts I received from Frank was the reminder to keep relationships current and in good shape—fate can come down and zap me at any time. And you.

Ask yourself, if your Frank were to die tomorrow, how would you feel about your relationships—about everything? Are you in balance? Have you left things unsaid that you will never be able to say again to the person who needs to hear it?

Then look beyond. The person who died—what were his, or her, "undone" things? We are all so busy taking care of unimportant things, things that seem important, but in actuality are not. It's a reality and problem with most of us. Frank left some things "undone" with his father as well as his step-father. The unsaids of yesterday. Today ended. Tomorrow didn't hold another day for him. There weren't any more opportunities left to finish his business. There won't be opportunities to finish your "leftovers" either.

In discovering your spiritual vision, let your eyes be opened to the truly important things in life. Those things which hold significance. Real significance. You may not be able to change your *why*, but you can change your world.

### The Next Step . . .

A shining example of this kind of spiritual vision is found in Jonathan Hunter, who has shared his story with millions. I connected with him through mutual contacts with "The 700 Club." Jonathan was a top male model, posing for magazines like *Gentleman's Quarterly* and living a fast lifestyle. He tried everything, including drugs and homosexuality. Jonathan's rapid pace continued until, one day, he was stopped in his tracks. Three days after snorting enough PCP to kill three people (he said he thought it was cocaine), Jonathan knew that something—Someone—had saved him from death. It was then that Jonathan welcomed God into his life. At first he didn't think that included giving up his "gay" lifestyle. Soon, though, he realized that the way he was living was not consistent with what he was reading in the Bible. He realized that he wasn't homosexual, but he was a heterosexual struggling with homosexual tendencies. He came face to face with his need to change.

Tragically, in 1985, after making a total turnabout in his lifestyle, Jonathan discovered that he tested positive to the AIDS antibody. Persistent questions crowded his mind. How long would it be before this disease took over his body? Would God ever heal him? *Could* God ever heal him? And why now, when he had finally made a total commitment to God, did God allow him to get this disease?

One thing was sure—in spite of his questions, Jonathan had to begin living one day at a time. It was through his *whys*—through the prospect of facing death—that a spiritual vision was birthed. Jonathan began an outreach to other AIDS victims, first through prayer, then through consistent visitation, until now he heads a ministry called ARM: AIDS Resource Ministry. Rather than fall prey to his *whys,* Jonathan turned them around to a *why not? Why not* help others? *Why not* make his life count? *Why not* change the things he could change? Jonathan's *no* has become his mission in life—a great big *YES* to help others! In the meantime, he still hopes and believes that God will heal him. His positive faith, his spiritual vision, has carried him through many difficult questions and opened the door for others to find comfort in the loving arms of God.

## Visions . . . Past . . . and Present

One of the most powerful spiritual visions can be seen in the garden of Gethsemane where Jesus pled with God to change the plan. Did He indeed *have* to go to the cross to fulfill God's purpose? Wasn't there another way? Surely there was a better way. God's answer came back. *No.* There wasn't.

The Bible tells us that Jesus endured the pain along with the shame and humiliation of crucifixion because He could see beyond the cross—He could see the glorious plan of God that would unfold through His profound suffering. This spiritual vision carried Him through. He could see that behind God's *no* there lay a resounding *yes* for all of humanity. *Yes* I love you. *Yes* I will hear your prayers and answer you. *Yes* I will forgive all your sins. *Yes* I will embrace you and give you entrance into heaven where you will never again cry or be afraid, or be victimized or be sick or lonely or hungry or suffer again through the innumerable indignities this life can offer. Whether you are old or young, rich or poor, no matter what you have suffered, this is a spiritual vision that anyone can grasp—that will carry you through life with certainty and assurance.

Responsibility comes when a vision is birthed, not only responsibility to God, but also your responsibility to fellow human beings—to those who need what only you can offer in terms of comfort, understanding and empathy. The Bible warns us that to whom much is given, much is required. And truly, when you think of what God requires, it's not a harsh, demanding assignment; it's a loving, simple request.

What does God require? The answer is simple and contained poignantly in the words of Micah 6:8 (KJV), "What doth the Lord require of thee, but to do justly, and to love mercy, and to walk humbly with thy God?" Amen!

To do justly: to be fair, honest, upright, responsible, kind-hearted. To love mercy: to remember your own short-comings, your own failures, your own weaknesses and to be aware that you are every bit as capable of evil and injustice as the next person. To walk humbly with God: to understand that God in His great mercy toward you has forgiven you so much that you have no reason to boast of anything.

Everything we have has been given to us freely by the hand of God. Our greatest responsibility is to take the tremendous blessing of life and to live that life fully, giving and serving others.

There's a belief these days that happiness and fulfillment will come by "finding" ourselves. The fallacy in this viewpoint is that when we search for "me," when we do as Frank Sinatra sang, "I did it my way," we're stuck with the triviality of what we find. Because the truth is, what we are is not much—it's what we give that becomes great.

One person put it this way. If all I am is forgiven when I go to heaven, then everything in my life will have been forgotten, because God promises to forget our sins and not to remember them any more. But if I stand before God, not only having been forgiven in this life, but also having loved, then I bring a great reward with me into heaven.

As I put the finishing touches on this manuscript, my community is in shock. More than a month has passed since Tuesday, October 17, 1989, 5:04 P.M. Pacific Coast Time. My community is attempting to assess the damage—emotional, physical, material, and for some, even spiritual—of the recent earthquake.

The media have focused on two areas. The Marina District of San Francisco and the collapse of the section of Interstate 880 in Oakland. That looks like the "big stuff." But is it?

Throughout the Bay Area of Northern California, there is tremendous damage. Some towns have, by all definition, been demolished. They may not look it at first glance, but reality will set in when the demolition crews arrive within a few days.

Wonderful cities like Los Gatos and Santa Cruz will never be the same. As they were, they no longer are. Watsonville is now a tent city. Parts of San Francisco that never made the news—they weren't on fire—are literally going to be demolished. Homes in the Haight Ashbury and Richmond areas will be torn down. Not big stuff for TV. But big stuff for the residents.

As they learned their homes and businesses were to be no longer, residents were advised that they had fifteen minutes to get out what they wanted, what they needed. And then they might never enter the premises again, for the cranes and tractors—the demolition crews—arrived shortly. Fifteen minutes. Where do you begin? What do you leave? What do you take? At first thought, you might say that nothing needs to be cleaned up. But is that true?

Most of us are scatterers—leaving bits and pieces of debris here and there, sometimes not finishing any one thing. Fifteen minutes. Where do you start? Where do you end? What do you leave? What do you take?

In allowing the nonessentials to drop, the nonessentials that would never be included in your fifteen-minute dash, you create an enormous opening. It's the vision—your spiritual vision—that becomes an incredible gift. It's a gift that begins to sort out, to get things—your life, fears, hopes and dreams—into perspective.

When you find a spiritual vision, when you pursue it with all your heart, when you reach out to become what God has created you to be, when you offer to others the lessons you have learned in this life, you will then find the answer to your pain. It won't be a reason for your suffering, but a purpose. A spiritual vision will carry you through the many trials of this life.

No one is exempt from pain. No one is exempt from problems. No one is exempt from being human. It's our common fate—a common part of humanity. Conversely, anyone is in a position to help, to give of self. Life is filled with opportunity to find happiness just by living for giving.

I know that the tragedies, the pain and the suffering I have experienced are not things I would choose if I had a choice. But I didn't, and I know it. I do know, however, that I can help others. I have felt their hurts and their joys. I have lived and am very much alive. And so are you. What separates us from others is that willingness to give so freely, unselfishly. It comes with vision—for and of ourselves, of others and of God.

# 8

# Miracles Do Happen!

■     ■     ■

**M**y three years were almost up. I could hardly wait to end my term on the ruling board of my church. A lot had happened over the three years—major changes, major upheavals, major pain as well as a continued probe and expansion of my own spirituality.

At the last session meeting, just prior to Thanksgiving, we all went around the room sharing what we were thankful for. If I had received the letter from the foster child John and I had taken in the year before, prior to that meeting, I would have shared it. By the following Sunday, though, the letter was in my hands and I was able to share it with the entire congregation as I made my last presentation for our stewardship drive.

The girl who wrote the letter was thirteen going on thirty-three when she came into our lives. The year before, John and I, unsuspecting of the roles we were about to play, had left church and stopped by our friend Cathy's home to pick up a video. Her granddaughter, whom I had known since she was a little tyke, had been having teen problems, big ones, at home.

Now, almost by definition, teens have problems. Kristie appeared to have an extra dose. Her handling of her problems, herself and her interactions with her family and school, were definitely not acceptable. She

had become a one-person anti-everything. School. Society. Family. The previous Christmas, she had spent
the holidays in Juvenile Hall. She had stolen material
items, money, credit cards; she had been drinking and
using pot. Her grandmother had taken her in, but unknown to John and me, was about at the end of her
rope, too.

After our usual greetings I innocently asked Cathy
if she had seen a certain movie. She hadn't. I suggested
we all go and take Kristie with us. "Kristie's not going
anywhere," snapped Cathy.

Something was pretty wrong here. The storm
unfolded. Kristie was drinking and couldn't be trusted
for anything. Cathy had caught her sneaking back in
after a "night" out. Kristie had made her own life
miserable, and now she was making everyone else's
life miserable as well.

Cathy had had it. She would not be lied to any
more. The pain of her own daughter's death due to
drugs was overwhelming. When she saw her granddaughter heading down the same path as Lori had, she
couldn't bear it—she would do anything to help Kristie
through this period. And yet, here was Kristie, telling
the same lies and stories as Lori did.

It was deja vu. The nightmare for my friend continued. She was throwing in the towel. She had done
all she could do with the tools she had. She felt Kristie
needed something, but she apparently wasn't that
something.

Instead of just picking up the video, we stayed for
dinner. Since our ten-minute stopover was going to last
a few hours, I decided to go and take a quick glance at
the video. Kristie followed me into the bedroom and
crawled on the bed with me. My first words were, "You

really blew it, didn't you?" Her response was, "The others made me do it."

I couldn't believe what she said—the others made her do it! For the next two hours, I talked with Kristie, confronting her gently, sometimes not so gently. If she was ever going to get her act together, taking responsibility for herself was a key ingredient.

Before she went to bed that night, John recited to her the poem about courage from Winnie the Pooh. It ends by saying, "Don't give up hope." She made promises. Kristie seemed encouraged.

Her family wasn't though—they were at their wit's end with that girl. And I couldn't blame them. We knew what it was like—we had gone through the drug routine with one of my kids. It was hell for us—John and I took turns sleeping at night. We didn't know if we would have a house standing the next morning if we both slept.

Our ten-minute stopover that started at six P.M. went on to one A.M. We talked with Cathy and Kristie. Mostly, we listened. One of my best friends was hurting enormously. I hated to see her so torn, so vulnerable. Cathy was going to call Kristie's probation officer the next day; if Kristie went to a foster home, that was her problem, her choice. Cathy could do no more.

Both John and I hated to see Kristie go to a foster home, but that's where she was definitely headed. We hated to see her rough and tumbled around by the system, and we were convinced that it would not be the solution to her problems. Late into that evening and early morning we talked. Perhaps if we took her in for a few weeks, things would slow down. Get better. If it would take the pressure off Cathy, then maybe Kristie could move back in with her.

That's not how the system worked. We couldn't take her for a couple of weeks—we had to either take her for five or six months or not at all. And we had to be approved as foster parents by the county. Finally, we felt there was no choice. We knew we had to do it.

I called Cathy the next morning and asked her if she had an hour—that I would be over in fifteen minutes. Upon arriving, I drove her to a school that had done wonders for two of my kids—turn-arounds for them both—one who was quite dyslexic and the other who had entered the drug scene.

Both had graduated, were whole human beings, had done major about-faces. After meeting with the principal and a counselor, I asked Cathy if she would be willing to pay fall tuition for the private school if John and I agreed to be Kristie's foster parents. Never hesitating, she said she would.

Having gone through it with our kids we knew what we were in for. Rules had to be made. And kept. We were willing to let Kristie come if both she and her family agreed to our rules: she would have to go to the school of our choice; she would not be in contact with her parents for thirty days; she would have to go to the therapist of our choice, a therapist who had helped John and me restore our marriage as well as someone who specialized in chemical abuse by teens; she would go to church with us; she would have to go to work for me. And my staff had to be behind her being there one hundred percent—if I were away on business, they in fact became surrogate foster mothers; her family would have to put new locks on our home so it was both break-in and break-out proof. Booze and drugs do a lot of talking—and we weren't about to listen.

The night before Kristie officially arrived on our doorstep, she attempted suicide. The day before she had learned that she would be living with us; she had also learned the day before that she was going to a new therapist, the therapist of our choice. Both were fine with her. What she hadn't been told by her parents and grandmother was that she would not be going to the same school. A new one, a school of my choice, was her only option.

Kristie was furious. Her reaction was to drink the wine she had stashed and to cut her wrists. She then called me after the deed was done. I, in turn, called the new therapist. How Cathy stayed uninvolved, almost oblivious to Kristie's trauma/drama unfolding in another part of her home, I'm not sure. But she did.

When Kristie called me and told me of her "deed," I was able to determine that her cuts were not physically life threatening. I had her talk with the therapist and proceeded to have her bandaged up. The next morning, we both went to the therapist together after I had Kristie take the massage I had scheduled for myself that morning. Somehow, I felt that stroking and touching would be something she needed.

Between the mental doctor, the medical doctor, the touch doctor and me, the caring doctor, we made it through that first day, the first week. Kristie's cutting of her wrists was not effective enough to take her life. It was, though, effective in saying she needed help— plenty of it.

It was great, at least in the beginning. For the first few months, Kristie was in love with me. We restored some privileges as time passed. She started doing well in school. And she started to make new friends. I must add that in spite of her improvements, things were not as smooth as I thought they would be. Kristie's presence created havoc with my oldest daughter, Shelley, who was sure we were suffering from "empty nest syndrome" and out of our minds for bringing this problem into our home, our lives. I was not prepared, nor did I ever anticipate, that I would be confronted with sibling rivalry at this stage of my life. After all, my daughters were twenty-four and twenty. But that's what it was.

Shelley wasn't happy that Kristie was firmly entrenched in our home. It's not that Kristie had taken over her old room or used any of her things, at least not directly. What Kristie had done was this: She had possessed us. John and I couldn't do anything without making plans for Kristie—she went everywhere with us. Or, we stayed home and had friends over. Our friends supported us in supporting Kristie . . . and our attempt to help her.

Honeymoons don't last forever. Ours was no exception. For many parents of teens, there is often the "lull before the storm." Four months after Kristie arrived, we allowed her to stay overnight with one of her school friends. We had a phone number, names of parents. I even called the school to ask about the other girl and her family. John and I looked forward to being with each other, a night off we both felt we had earned.

A few weeks later, Kristie asked again if she could stay over and go to a barbecue. After checking with parents and about the barbecue host, we found that all did not fit! We didn't get a one-plus-one equation. It was full of fractions. I called her mother and suggested that we have a physical checkup on her—I was suspicious of drugs.

One of our initial rules was that if there was any doubt on my part, Kristie would have to go to Alcoholics Anonymous and/or Narcotics Anonymous. Attendance at these meetings would be the consequence of what John and I deemed suspicious behavior—no real proof was needed. If we said she had to go, she had to go. Her therapist backed us up.

Miss Kristie tested positive and I knew that meeting time was in order. There were several locations and times to choose from. Most meetings were held at local churches in our immediate area. Originally, I hadn't planned to attend these meetings, but here I found myself weekly, sitting with Kristie in a smoke-filled room. My allergies crawled up the walls to escape the smell of the smoke. She fought going in the first place—but we reminded her of the rules, the rules that she okayed in the first place. The rules that she, and only she, chose to break.

Approximately six months after Kristie arrived, she went home—always the primary goal for her family and for us. All of them had been in therapy—sometimes alone, sometimes together for the past six months. They had learned a lot about each other. There was still more to come. But they were talking to each other—a major breakthrough.

At one point Kristie's suicide attempt had had me calling for help while I was nursing her wounds and trying to keep her alive, wondering if I was out of my mind. So that Thanksgiving, after her letter arrived, I knew that all the hassles and trials of trying to get Kristie to straighten out, of trying to make a difference in her life, had been worth it. "Thank you for saving my life," she wrote. Kristie had been resurrected! The probation department was pleased with her progress.

So were her parents and her therapist. That's what caring and sharing are all about. That's what being a human being is all about.

### Super Scary

"Miracle on I-880" trumpeted my Sunday newspaper headlines. October 17, 1989, will be a day that Bay Area residents won't forget. For rescue workers dismantling the span of freeway known as I-880 in Oakland, California, a miracle surfaced four days after the earthquake. No one expected anyone to be alive who had been trapped under the collapse of the California Interstate Freeway. Especially as more days passed.

As rescue workers broke up a concrete coffin, one thought he saw a hand move in one of the crushed cars. They burrowed fifteen feet through the concrete and eventually pulled Buck Helm from his tomb. He had been there for ninety hours! When word spread that someone had been found alive, everyone's demeanor changed. People walked faster, stronger. Smiles even surfaced. Rescue workers double-checked other areas, hoping to find more survivors. Buck Helm lived for thirty-one days after the quake, finally succumbing to heart disease, not the injuries from the bridge collapse. His survival during that time created an atmosphere of hope and healing. And of faith for many.

Buck Helm's chances of survival were zero. The doctors said he was a miracle man. Rather, it was his will to live, the human spirit. Was it—or was there more?

I was speaking at the American College of Surgeons in Atlanta, Georgia, when news came that San Francisco had been hit by a major earthquake. I rushed back to my room to find a message from my daughter —she and Frankie were OK. I couldn't reach home or my other daughter, since the phone lines were down. Throughout the night, I was glued to the TV.

The screen and telecasters kept talking about the Marina District fire in San Francisco—a fire that would destroy an entire block. Homes were no longer homes. A portion of the Bay Bridge had collapsed.

I was worried and horribly frustrated. There was hardly a mention of the rest of the area. The epicenter was in Santa Cruz—I live closer to Santa Cruz than to San Francisco. San Francisco was 100 miles from the epicenter—why was there no news? Why didn't the local news feed into the national networks? Why didn't they get in their traffic watch helicopters and fly down toward Santa Cruz and find what other damage existed?

Later that evening, the horror of I-880 was unveiled—a major freeway destroyed. No one could imagine after seeing those pictures that a Buck Helm could have survived for any period of time trapped as he was for four days. No one can conceive of the extraction of the little boy who had to have his leg primitively amputated in the car while his dead mother lay inches away.

The doctors gave young Julio Berumen an excellent prognosis. They expected him to walk out of the hospital with an artificial leg. He did, just before Christmas. His sister, also trapped in the car, is home after undergoing many hours of reconstructive surgery. The community had collected over $150,000 to help support and educate the Berumen children. Their father had heard the news of the quake on TV as he watched the World Series. When he heard of the freeway collapse, he was alarmed. He knew his family might be on it. When the news aired that two children, a girl eight and a boy six, had been pulled from the wreckage, he just knew that they were his. Cathy and Julio were the only survivors of the collapsed section of Interstate 880. Their mother had died instantly.

All I could think of was just how bad was it. Estimates of damage were initially one to two billion dollars. No way, my mind said. Rather, it's billions more. What about the surrounding communities? And what about all my friends? And what about my family? I never even thought about my house—was it still standing or was it trashed like so many?

My daughter again got through to me six hours after the initial quake. My grandson said, "Super scary, Mama. Super scary." She was OK and had connected with my other daughter. No one could find John. He got through the following day and informed me of some of the damages—all fixable.

Two days out, still little had been said about surrounding communities. Is this nuts—how could such a big quake, 7.1 on the Richter Scale, bypass cities and towns immediately surrounding the epicenter? My common sense was going crazy.

Three days later, I flew home. San Francisco Airport was a mess. The quake had jarred the ceiling sprinklers and flooded the terminal I was in. By the third day the moldy, damp smell was overwhelming; the ceiling was down. More news came in—major destruction all over the area. Santa Cruz, Watsonville and Los Gatos would virtually have to be rebuilt.

Cities?! Where was the massive media coverage? These people needed money—billions of dollars. They needed blankets, tents, clothes, food. The fire and destruction of homes in San Francisco was horrible, but it was just a small part of nature's overall blow.

When I first wrote this chapter, it was shortly after the earthquake in Northern California in 1989. The news media had played the disaster and damage to the hilt. Financial damage was many billions of dollars— personal trauma, there's no price tag. And it wasn't even the *big one!*

Yet in all the chaos, in all the damage and uncertainty, God is here. God didn't cause the destruction. He did, however, cause, to some, an aftershock. As I watched Hurricane Hugo's fury only a few weeks earlier I was appalled at the amount of looting and noncaring for others and their properties. San Francisco was wide open, as were Santa Cruz, Los Gatos, Watsonville, Hollister, Oakland, and other cities. Yet wonder of wonders, the kind of behavior that was Hugo's aftermath was literally nonexistent in Northern California in October of 1989.

The people of Northern California rose to the occasion. Some were barely dressed. Many were homeless. Some had lost friends and loved ones. They forgot themselves and put on a sensational performance to help others. God moves people to do generous things in the midst of chaos. He helps us to restore our human dignity.

When Hugo hit, the residents of Santa Cruz raised thousands of dollars to send to Charleston, South Carolina, to help their rebuilding process. In San Francisco, residents rolled up their sleeves and ran with hoses to the ocean, many blocks away from where the actual fire was. Concerns for themselves didn't exist. Concern for others did.

Since the first edition of this book, there have been countless "natural" disasters in the world. It seems as if California has had more than its share. Fires, floods, and more earthquakes. The quake that hit the Los Angeles area in January 1994 collapsed several free-ways, started fires, demolished apartments, homes, buildings—even hospitals were destroyed. Tent cities erupted throughout Southern California.

The financial devastation is in the mega billions of dollars. The emotional costs—who knows? In the early nineties, for the first time in decades, California exported more people than the number of people who moved there. For many, the land of golden opportunity has become the land of fear. As a native Californian who lived there for over forty years and exited in 1990, I can now count more friends who have moved from the state than remain. Times have certainly changed, and many seem to have lost hope.

Is hope dead? Or is it merely on the sidelines? For many, it is neither. Southern California is rebuilding. Those who make it their home rolled up their sleeves to help others. "Neighbors," individuals and families who had never met before the quake, found their bricked property-line separation walls knocked down by it. A common meal, a wheelbarrow, a helping hand became the norm. Some rebuilt the walls—others chose to keep them down.

### God's Work

This is God at work. These are the miracles that are birthed. God doesn't send calamities, the misfortunes of life that all of us experience at some time. He does, however, give us—you and me—the ability to cope, to handle it. When uncertainty permeates the air, con-fronting us at what appears to be every corner, there is one thing to do. Pray. God is with us. If the eventual outcome of our uncertainty, of our despair, is good news, we should be grateful. If it's not, know and trust that God will give you the inner tools to survive.

Churches throughout the Bay Area of Northern California were packed the weekend after the quake with those who gave thanks, with those who prayed for others . . . and for themselves. There is no question in my mind that the thousands of others injured prayed and asked for God's help in those dark moments—those moments of chaos, uncertainty, and fear after the earthquake.

### Life Is a Resurrection

For me, sharing Christ's glory, sharing in His resurrection power, is sharing in the resurrection of a person's life. With spiritual vision, miracles do and will happen. Behind every *no* is a *yes*; even a surprise—like Kristie. When we recognize a fraction of what God is doing in and for us, the pains and hurts that are felt are lessened, and even made to fade as the spiritual vision shapes the tomorrows. When I think about miracles, I don't think about all the hoopla that goes along with glorious healings, miraculous rescues. I think of the little miracles in life—the little miracles that are actually the biggest part of life. To have a great life—that's a miracle. To have a sense of peace—that's a miracle. To survive an ordeal such as a major disaster is a miracle. Miracles show us what is possible, not what is impossible.

The resurrection of Jesus happened only once. It will never happen again. But life is full of little resurrections. There are lots of deaths as we go through life—the death of a loved one, the death of a dream, the death of a relationship, the death of our health, the death of our physical safety through a fire or through a rape or through a murder—death surrounds us. Yet in the midst of all this death, there's a miracle—the miracle of a resurrection. The miracle of life. The miracle that happens when the tragedies of failure and suffering become the fertile ground for a new start, a new life. That miracle has to occur internally—within one's own soul and spirit.

Following a death or a tragedy, you may be surrounded with other people. But eventually, they have to get on with their own lives. Eventually, you have to reach inside yourself and find your own reason to go on living. Your own answers to your own *whys*. Your own *yeses* behind your own *noes*. Your own faith and your own spiritual vision. God gives each one of us the tools to help ourselves. God helps us to get unstuck.

When I was driving home from the airport, when my church was going through some of the problems I shared with you, to have the incredible feeling of God's arms wrapping around me—that was a miracle. God was real! Alive! Touchable!

After Frank died, my sister-in-law came with her little girl, Shelby. Fourteen years have passed since Frank died, yet to this day, I thank God for Linda bringing Shelby when she flew in from Colorado. I praise Him for the miracle of life that forces you to stay in touch, not slip back and get in the crevice of darkness. Who can allow themselves to be so immersed in pain when there is an active, happy child around? For me, Shelby was a miracle. One that I needed.

## Life Is for the Living

A miracle is a celebration—a celebration of life. My husband, John, used to hate holidays. He came from an unhappy home, an alcoholic mother, a noncaring family. He was always amazed at the festivities and the joy of planning that went into our holidays, whether it was Christmas or a birthday.

Frank's death fell on September 3—John's birthday. But it was also the first day of the Labor Day weekend. John needed his birthday back. We needed to celebrate life on his birthday, not death. We needed a miracle of resurrection. Now, to this day, I refer to Frank's death as being on Labor Day. John's birthday will always be on September 3. He is very much alive. I go out of my way to celebrate his day. Whether it's just us, or friends, it's his day. This is life continuing—and it's a miracle.

Celebrating life in all its forms is one of my supremest pleasures, my greatest joys. I love to entertain, having friends over. Setting my table is one of life's simple pleasures—it's an art to me. It can be very simplistic or very ornate. A pot of geraniums. Mustard seeds. Whatever. Just so I'm celebrating life—celebrating resurrection. A celebration that's a miracle and a celebration acknowledging how important my friends are to me. I want them to know this when they are alive. Flowers and words won't register, at least not for them, when they are dead.

The older I get, the more simple I become. You will never see me driving a Mercedes again. I don't need to feel good about myself by surrounding myself with expensive toys for everyone else's benefit. For the first time in my life we bought a used van, somebody else's. I'm so tickled with us, we have broken the "need" to have the best, whatever one defines as the best. Instead, we have what we really need, not what somebody else thinks we need. We are free—that's a miracle.

My grandson is another miracle. He was named

after Frank. At three, Frankie was such a gift. Every day he would remind me, "Mama, your darling boy is here." Today, I easily respond to Mama, Grandma, Gram, Ma, or just about anything his voice is connected to.

As I pen this edition of *When God Says No,* Frankie has just celebrated his ninth birthday. What would my husband and I do without him? One of our birthday gifts was his first dog—an American Eskimo bundle of white fur he named Sasha. Sasha's namesake is from the *Star Trek: The Next Generation* series.

Both Frankie and Papa—his name for my husband, John—are avid Trekkers. Oh, I confess, I enjoy it too, although I do not go to the Star Trek conventions like the two of them do. Frankie wanted to name his new puppy after someone, a female, in the series. Neither Counselor Troi nor Dr. Crusher were the right fit. Then we remembered that the head of security on the spaceship *U.S.S. Enterprise* before Lieutenant Worf was a blond—Tasha Yar. Seems perfect—one of Tasha's responsibilities is to be part of our household security. Tasha became Sasha.

Does Frankie have me wrapped around his little finger? You bet. I'd do anything, *anything,* for this child. He turns me into Jell-O. Frankie is such an incredible joy to both John and me. A true celebration. A miracle? Without a doubt.

When you find yourself tempted, as Frank did when he was six years old, to say, "Life is too long, too hard and unfair," take a moment to stop. Reflect on the powerful messages found in everyday life. And often the most powerful are the most simple.

The joys and sounds of Christmas are among my greatest pleasures. The music of the season fills the air with both spiritual and modern renderings. One of my quasi-modern favorites is found in the movie, *White Christmas*, which is peppered with Irving Berlin's music. He shares this simple message in song for meeting life's problems: "When I'm worried and I can't sleep, I count my blessings instead of sheep, and I fall asleep counting my blessings."

Today I am rich with blessings. I have my health and I have my family. I have been rich. And I have been poor, very poor, as in welfare type of poor. I have had great bouts of sickness, pain, disasters. Yet I am blessed. I have had a good life.

God reminds us that it's never hopeless. There's always, always—in the midst of heartache and tragedy— a blessing to remember, to find. A blessing to focus our minds on. A miracle—the miracle of life. Let's live it together and show the world what life is really all about. God doesn't send disasters our way. He does, though, send a miracle—His *yes* is that ability to cope with it. Once tragedy, disaster, or misfortune strikes, use it as your personal eye-opening experience to learn, to stretch, to grow.

Life includes the gift of spirituality, finding solace in a God who loves us. It's about becoming a little kid again—Frank's final gift to me. It's about allowing God to envelop us. And it's about emerging from a cocoon and becoming a butterfly, a butterfly who is delighted with life and the discovery of its beauty. And it's about joy—that deep settled confidence that God is in control. Knowing that God is in control, I can be in control.

And last, it's knowing who we are. That life has meaning and purpose—that there's a reason for my life, your life. Your life can and will count for something more than just a momentary passage through this world. And your life holds the potential to touch others, to change them—and will add something good and positive in the continuum of this universe. You matter, infinitely, to those around you—and to God. With God's assurance of order, you will find a place to return to, to replenish your strength, your hope, your love, you.

As I close this book, my prayer for you is not that all your *whys* have been answered. They aren't going to be. Rather, move away from *why* and be ready for your *yes*. Somewhere, out there, it's ready to drop in. My prayer is that you will take a look inside yourself, view the future, your future, and find your reason to live, to be here.

Pain is inevitable . . . misery is not. Some of my speaker friends have queried me as to why I love life, why I love to laugh, why I always try to find the good side of any situation. The answer is really simple. It's Frank's little kid/fun spirit he left with me. I'm willing to work enormously hard, put in long hours, but there's got to be fun. And that's part of the joy of life. I truly believe the amount of pain and agony I've experienced is directly parallel to the amount of joy I can feel and can give. One's cup of joy can only be as deep as one's sorrow.

Why am I so joyful? Because I've gone through so much. Will I have more negative experiences? Probably. But with the tools I have, my love of God, my comfort in my spirituality, my sense of fun and knowledge of who I am and what I'm about, any obstacle can be overcome. *All my noes have led to yeses. Even miracles.*

Since I was a little girl—over fifty years ago—I have been an avid reader of Ann Landers and Dear Abby. For years, I clipped articles and tracked down books and poems that were cited. Recently, a column introduced me to the writings of Henry Van Dyke. In his *A Parable of Immortality*, he eloquently addresses the earthly departure of a loved one. Let me share his words with you.

> I am standing upon the seashore. A ship at my side spreads her white sails to the morning breeze and starts for the ocean. She is an object of beauty and strength, and I watch until at last she hangs like a speck of white cloud just where the sun and sky come down to mingle. Then someone says, "There she goes!"
>
> Gone where? Gone from my sight—that is all. She is just as large in mast and hull and spar as she was when she left my side and just as able to bear her load of living freight to their destination.
>
> Her diminished size is in me, not in her. And just at the moment when someone at my side says, "There she goes!" other eyes watch her coming and other voices take up the shout, "Here she comes!"

After Frank died, I felt horribly alone—deserted. Somehow, the nineteen years he sailed were diminished, as if they never counted. There were times I felt that they were not experienced. A dream. Today I realize that I had nineteen years of memories. Some as huge as a white mast; others, a mere speck on the horizon.

You and everyone you know will experience rough times. No one has an exclusive on good times, a perfect or charmed life. Each of us will undergo *noes*. When they occur, stop. You don't have the luxury to get stuck on *why*. Why begets why begets why. Stop. Get ready to move on. To be ready for the *yes* that is coming your way. You are one of God's gifts. His miracles. The final step and completion of His cycle.

# *Epilogue*

In the last chapter, I wrote that pain is inevitable, misery is not, that when you hit the bad times—the potholes of life—choices must be made. You can choose to sink and drown or learn to swim. My choice is to swim, fully aware that there will be more potholes down the road. I tell my audiences that the person I am today is not the result of the successes that I have had—and there have been plenty—but the result of the disasters, failures, mistakes, and pain that I have endured and grown from. Strength through adversity. *Yeses* from *noes.*

*When God Says No* was first published in 1990. Since then, I have had letters and phone calls and have been approached by strangers wanting and needing to reach out. To be touched. To be assured that there is hope. Bad things, bad times, bad people are all too common. Today's violence, the disintegration of family life, the decline of values, and the bombarding negativity make one want to exit, stage right.

Don't. You count, tremendously. You have seen that I have traveled many paths, some of them extremely painful—mentally, spiritually, physically, even materially. I know you have too. You do not fail because of the mistakes or disasters exposed by the path you are on.

You only fail when you quit trying. For whatever reason you have this book in your hands, in your thoughts, in your heart, there is a reason. We are in this together. There is a YES.

**Judith Briles, Ph.D.,** is a motivational speaker with substance, a best-selling author of fifteen books, and is nationally recognized as an expert in solutions to women's issues. She is known as a catalyst for change and believes that every pitfall experience leads to an opportunity for greater success.

Her books include *The Confidence Factor, The Briles Report on Women in Healthcare, Woman to Woman, Gendertraps, Money Sense, Financial Savvy for Women, The Dollars and Sense of Divorce, Raising Money-Wise Kids,* and *Money Phases.* She co-authored *The Workplace: Questions Women Ask* with Lucy Swindoll and Mary Whelchel.

Dr. Briles's speaking and writing concentrate on commonsense strategies that can be adapted to both personal and workplace environments. To inquire about speaking and workshop availability or to subscribe to her quarterly newsletter, *The Woman's Voice,* contact the author at:

Dr. Judith Briles
P.O. Box 22021
Denver, CO 80222-0021
(303) 745-4590 or Fax (303) 745-4595
E-mail DrJBriles@aol.com